OPPOSING VIEWPOINTS®
The War on Drugs

Tamara L. Roleff, *Book Editor*

Bonnie Szumski, *Publisher*
Scott Barbour, *Managing Editor*
Helen Cothran, *Senior Editor*

OPPOSING
VIEWPOINTS®
SERIES

GREENHAVEN
PRESS ®

THOMSON
_____*_____
GALE

San Diego • Detroit • New York • San Francisco • Cleveland
New Haven, Conn. • Waterville, Maine • London • Munich

THOMSON
———✳———™
GALE

LIBRARY OF CONGRESS CATALOGING-IN-PUBLICATION DATA
The war on drugs : opposing viewpoints / Tamara L. Roleff, book editor.
    p. cm. — (Opposing viewpoints series)
Includes bibliographical references and index.
ISBN 0-7377-2285-1 (pbk. : alk. paper) — ISBN 0-7377-2284-3 (lib. : alk. paper)
    1. Narcotics, Control of—Government policy—United States. 2. Narcotics and crime—United States. 3. Drug abuse—Government policy—United States. 4. Drug abuse—United States—Prevention. 5. Crime and race—United States. 6. Terrorism—United States. 7. Drug legalization—United States. 8. United States—Social conditions. 9. United States—Politics and government. I. Roleff, Tamara L., 1959– . II. Opposing viewpoints series (Unnumbered)
HV5825.W381285 2004
363.45'0973—dc22   2003063063

Printed in the United States of America

ACC Library Services
Austin, Texas

"Congress shall make no law...abridging the freedom of speech, or of the press."

First Amendment to the U.S. Constitution

The basic foundation of our democracy is the First Amendment guarantee of freedom of expression. The Opposing Viewpoints Series is dedicated to the concept of this basic freedom and the idea that it is more important to practice it than to enshrine it.

Contents

Why Consider Opposing Viewpoints?

"The only way in which a human being can make some approach to knowing the whole of a subject is by hearing what can be said about it by persons of every variety of opinion and studying all modes in which it can be looked at by every character of mind. No wise man ever acquired his wisdom in any mode but this."

John Stuart Mill

In our media-intensive culture it is not difficult to find differing opinions. Thousands of newspapers and magazines and dozens of radio and television talk shows resound with differing points of view. The difficulty lies in deciding which opinion to agree with and which "experts" seem the most credible. The more inundated we become with differing opinions and claims, the more essential it is to hone critical reading and thinking skills to evaluate these ideas. Opposing Viewpoints books address this problem directly by presenting stimulating debates that can be used to enhance and teach these skills. The varied opinions contained in each book examine many different aspects of a single issue. While examining these conveniently edited opposing views, readers can develop critical thinking skills such as the ability to compare and contrast authors' credibility, facts, argumentation styles, use of persuasive techniques, and other stylistic tools. In short, the Opposing Viewpoints Series is an ideal way to attain the higher-level thinking and reading skills so essential in a culture of diverse and contradictory opinions.

In addition to providing a tool for critical thinking, Opposing Viewpoints books challenge readers to question their own strongly held opinions and assumptions. Most people form their opinions on the basis of upbringing, peer pressure, and personal, cultural, or professional bias. By reading carefully balanced opposing views, readers must directly confront new ideas as well as the opinions of those with whom they disagree. This is not to simplistically argue that everyone who reads opposing views will—or should—change his or her opinion. Instead, the series enhances readers' understanding of their own views by encouraging confrontation with opposing ideas. Careful examination of others' views can lead to the readers' understanding of the logical inconsistencies in their own opinions, perspective on why they hold an opinion, and the consideration of the possibility that their opinion requires further evaluation.

Evaluating Other Opinions

To ensure that this type of examination occurs, Opposing Viewpoints books present all types of opinions. Prominent spokespeople on different sides of each issue as well as well-known professionals from many disciplines challenge the reader. An additional goal of the series is to provide a forum for other, less known, or even unpopular viewpoints. The opinion of an ordinary person who has had to make the decision to cut off life support from a terminally ill relative, for example, may be just as valuable and provide just as much insight as a medical ethicist's professional opinion. The editors have two additional purposes in including these less known views. One, the editors encourage readers to respect others' opinions—even when not enhanced by professional credibility. It is only by reading or listening to and objectively evaluating others' ideas that one can determine whether they are worthy of consideration. Two, the inclusion of such viewpoints encourages the important critical thinking skill of objectively evaluating an author's credentials and bias. This evaluation will illuminate an author's reasons for taking a particular stance on an issue and will aid in readers' evaluation of the author's ideas.

It is our hope that these books will give readers a deeper understanding of the issues debated and an appreciation of the complexity of even seemingly simple issues when good and honest people disagree. This awareness is particularly important in a democratic society such as ours in which people enter into public debate to determine the common good. Those with whom one disagrees should not be regarded as enemies but rather as people whose views deserve careful examination and may shed light on one's own.

Thomas Jefferson once said that "difference of opinion leads to inquiry, and inquiry to truth." Jefferson, a broadly educated man, argued that "if a nation expects to be ignorant and free . . . it expects what never was and never will be." As individuals and as a nation, it is imperative that we consider the opinions of others and examine them with skill and discernment. The Opposing Viewpoints Series is intended to help readers achieve this goal.

David L. Bender and Bruno Leone,
Founders

Greenhaven Press anthologies primarily consist of previously published material taken from a variety of sources, including periodicals, books, scholarly journals, newspapers, government documents, and position papers from private and public organizations. These original sources are often edited for length and to ensure their accessibility for a young adult audience. The anthology editors also change the original titles of these works in order to clearly present the main thesis of each viewpoint and to explicitly indicate the opinion presented in the viewpoint. These alterations are made in consideration of both the reading and comprehension levels of a young adult audience. Every effort is made to ensure that Greenhaven Press accurately reflects the original intent of the authors included in this anthology.

Introduction

"Cannabis is substantially less harmful than alcohol and should be treated not as a criminal issue but as a social and public health issue."

—Pierre Claude Nolin, senator and chairman of the Canadian Senate Committee on Illegal Drugs

"Lax marijuana policies . . . [will invite] U.S. citizens into Canada for marijuana use and that will increase the likelihood that both U.S. citizens and Canadian citizens will bring back the Canadian marijuana across the border for distribution and sale."

—Asa Hutchinson, director, Drug Enforcement Administration

In 2001 an Ontario, Canada, court of appeals issued a ruling that stunned Canadians and Americans alike. The court ruled that Terry Parker, an epileptic, had the right to possess and smoke marijuana to ease the symptoms caused by his disease. The court ordered Canada's Parliament to rewrite its drug laws within twelve months to permit the use of marijuana. The following year, the Canadian government issued its Medical Marijuana Access Regulations (MMAR), which permitted doctors to issue certificates authorizing their patients' use of marijuana for medicinal purposes.

Two Canadian judges found problems with Canada's drug laws even after the MMAR guidelines were released, however. In January 2003, a judge in Windsor, Ontario, ruled that Canada now had essentially no laws prohibiting the possession of small amounts of marijuana for personal use since Parliament had not rewritten Canada's marijuana laws concerning recreational drug use as directed by the court of appeals. A week later, a superior court judge ruled that the regulations concerning medical marijuana were unconstitutional because the government did not provide a source for patients to get the drug. Ontario superior court justice Sidney Lederman wrote,

It's not fair to allow people to smoke medicinal marijuana, then force them to get the drug from the corner drug dealer, which is what the scheme effectively does. Laws which put seriously ill, vulnerable people in a position where they have to deal with the criminal underworld to obtain medicine they have been authorized to take violate the constitutional right to security of the person.

In response to these two rulings, Health Canada implemented an application process for patients to grow their own supply of marijuana. In addition, the Cannabis Reform Bill was introduced into the House of Commons in May 2003. Under the proposed bill, possession of small amounts of marijuana would be decriminalized, with the penalty equivalent to a traffic ticket. Possession of more than thirty grams of marijuana and trafficking in or production of the drug would remain illegal, punishable by fines and incarceration. Parliament is expected to vote on the bill in the fall of 2003.

The Bush administration is sharply critical of Canada's efforts to decriminalize marijuana. John Walters, director of the White House Office of National Drug Control Policy (ONDCP), fears that Canada's liberalized drug laws will lead to that country becoming a major supplier of America's marijuana, which will undermine U.S. efforts to clamp down on illegal drug use. He contends that the United States already has a problem with marijuana being smuggled into the United States from Canada. He argues, "Right now we're being inundated with high-potency marijuana. When it's more available, when there's less social pressure not to use it, you get more use and in this case with these substances it produces more dependence." Walters warns that decriminalizing marijuana will lead to increased drug abuse, and he asserts that marijuana "is the single biggest drug of addiction that we have to provide treatment resources for. It's 60 percent of the problem. It's twice as important as cocaine. Americans don't appreciate this enough and I fear Canadians don't either."

Furthermore, Walters warns that decriminalizing marijuana in Canada could lead to various problems at the border. If marijuana is made more readily available in Canada, he reasons, there will be more attempts to smuggle the drug across the border into the United States. In consequence, he asserts, U.S. Customs officials will have to step up inspections at U.S.-Canadian border crossings, resulting in longer waits to enter the country. After hearing that a parliamentary committee recommended decriminalizing marijuana, Walters told reporters,

> It's not my job to judge Canadian policy. But it is my job to protect Americans from dangerous threats, and right now Canada is a dangerous staging area for some of the most potent and dangerous marijuana at a time when marijuana is the single biggest source of dependency-production in the United States. That's a problem. We have to make security at the border tougher because this is a dangerous threat to our young people and it makes the problem of patrolling the border more difficult.

Another problem is that as the United States increases border inspections to prevent drug smuggling, export shipments will likely be held up at the border, which will have a negative impact on trade and Canada's economy.

Most Canadians and U.S. supporters of relaxed drug laws scoff at claims that a liberalization of Canada's drug laws will result in increased drug activity in the United States and border problems. They point out that twelve U.S. states have drug laws that are as liberal as Canada's proposed marijuana law and neighboring states do not report increased drug use or border problems.

Keith Martin, a member of Parliament, argues that the American government should follow Canada's lead and soften its laws against drug use. He asserts that America's harsh drug laws do not reduce drug use. "The United States has the highest use of marijuana in the world with the most punitive drug laws," he points out. "That should tell them something. We know the status quo is a failure. The war on drugs has been a failure."

Martin and others believe that current Canadian laws that call for stiff jail sentences for possessing small amounts of marijuana for personal use are too draconian for such minor offenses. These harsh drug laws ruin the lives of thousands of young Canadians who are otherwise law-abiding citizens, they assert. Each year, about twenty thousand Canadians are prosecuted on marijuana possession charges. Under the proposed decriminalization law, most of those possession charges would be replaced with a fine equivalent to seventy-five U.S. dollars. Allan Rock, Canada's former health minister, asks, "Why clog the criminal courts with kids fourteen or fifteen who might have been experimenting with a single stick of marijuana and who could face a lifelong disadvantage with a criminal record? Isn't there a better way?" They contend that the resources of the criminal justice system should be focused on prosecuting more serious crimes.

Moreover, Canadians and drug war opponents argue that Canadian marijuana is not a major source of marijuana imported into the United States. U.S. customs records show that in 2002, slightly more than twenty thousand pounds of marijuana were seized at checkpoints along the U.S.-Canada border. In contrast, customs officials seized more than 1.2 million pounds of marijuana along the U.S.-Mexico border. The Royal Canadian Mounted Police estimate that the total amount of marijuana produced in Canada is about eight hundred tons. A 2003 report by the National Drug Intelligence Center states that the total supply of marijuana in the United States is between ten thousand and twenty-four thousand tons. Dan Gardner, a reporter for the Edmonton *Journal*, concludes, "Assuming Canada's annual pot crop really is 800 tons, it would make little difference to the U.S. supply even if every bud, leaf, and stem of Canadian pot were smuggled south."

The controversy over Canada's proposal to decriminalize marijuana illustrates the main arguments over the war on drugs. On the one hand are supporters of the drug war who contend that harsh drug laws are necessary to protect citizens from the dangers of drug abuse. On the other hand, opponents of the drug war claim that harsh drug laws are inhumane and the consequences of the laws outweigh any benefits they might provide. These arguments are among the issues debated in *The War on Drugs: Opposing Viewpoints*, which contains the following chapters: Is the War on Drugs Succeeding? Is There a Link Between the War on Drugs and Terrorism? Which Policies Are Working in the War on Drugs? Should Illegal Drugs Be Legalized? The authors in this anthology present a wide range of opinions on the many controversies surrounding the war on drugs.

CHAPTER 1

Is the War on Drugs Succeeding?

Chapter Preface

The United States has used military forces to fight the war on drugs almost from the official beginning of the war. American military forces are stationed along the U.S.-Mexican border to help Border Patrol and Customs officers apprehend drug smugglers. U.S. troops were also once stationed at Howard Air Force Base (AFB) in Panama (before U.S. control of the Panama Canal was returned to Panama in 1999). The troops performed more than two thousand missions each year, gathering intelligence on drug operations in Central and South America. Military surveillance planes flew over drug-producing countries such as Colombia and reported suspected drug production and trafficking to national police and military detachments, who then arrived to make the arrests. With the closing of Howard AFB, the United States needed to develop a new strategy for waging war on drug producers and traffickers in Central and South America. Eventually, the United States established a small military presence at airfields, known as Forward Operating Locations (FOLs), in Aruba, Curaçao, El Salvador, and Ecuador.

Supporters of FOLs assert that using scattered airfields offers several benefits. According to Barry McCaffrey, the former director of the Office of National Drug Control Policy, FOLs provide critical counternarcotics support to Central and South American nations. The strategically placed airfields allow U.S. military planes and military forces to reach an even larger area than was possible by using Howard AFB. In addition, using FOLs as opposed to a single U.S.-owned base is cost-effective. Because the airfields are owned by the host country, the annual operating cost for all the FOLs is about $20 million, about $55 million less than the budget was for Howard AFB.

Many are critical of America's use of FOLs in the U.S. war on drugs, however. Many residents of the host nations argue that permitting U.S. military forces on their soil amounts to imperialism—the practice of acquiring and then ruling a foreign nation. They contend that the FOLs are just a pretext to allow the United States to intervene in the host country's policies. According to GeorgeAnn Potter, a researcher and Latin America expert,

> Nobody in Latin America and the Caribbean thinks that U.S. military civic action programs are anything but intervention. With the fall of the Berlin Wall in 1989, the U.S. lost the pretext of "communism" for its intervention in Latin America and the Caribbean—other than Cuba—and it quickly assumed the "war on drugs" as an excuse for military presence.

In addition, opponents maintain that U.S. troops who train with the host countries' military forces are really trying to train them to work in the U.S. national interest, not their own country's interest.

Furthermore, opponents of FOLs argue that using military forces in the drug war is an inappropriate use of a valuable and costly resource. As commentator George Will states,

> The military's task is to deter war, and should deterrence fail, to swiftly and successfully inflict lethal violence on enemies. It is difficult enough filling an all-volunteer military with motivated warriors without blurring the distinction between military service and police work.

Many analysts are critical of the drug war in Central and South America generally. Donald Rumsfeld, secretary of defense under President George W. Bush, said in his confirmation hearing before the U.S. Senate in 2001 that he was not sure if the United States should spend $1.6 billion to fight the drug war in Colombia. "I am one who believes that the drug problem is probably overwhelmingly a demand problem, and that . . . if demand persists, it's going to find ways to get what it wants. And if it isn't from Colombia, it will be from someplace else."

Using the U.S. military to help perform interdiction to stop the drug supply into the United States is just one response to fighting the war on drugs. In the following chapter, the authors examine whether the war on drugs has been successful.

*"The fact is that our current policy,
balancing prevention, enforcement of our
laws, with treatment, have kept drug
usage outside the scope of acceptable
behavior in the United States."*

The War on Drugs Is Succeeding

Asa Hutchinson

Asa Hutchinson was formerly the director of the Drug Enforcement Administration (DEA). In the following viewpoint, excerpted from a speech he gave at Baylor University
in 2002, he asserts that the war on drugs is succeeding. He
contends that the war on drugs has reduced the demand for
illegal drugs by half. In addition, he rejects the claim that the
war is too draconian; he asserts that nearly all drug felons are
imprisoned for trafficking offenses, not for simply using or
possessing small amounts of illegal drugs. Hutchinson concludes that the war on drugs can be won as long as Americans do not give up the battle.

As you read, consider the following questions:
1. What is harm reduction, and how are some European
   cities implementing harm reduction programs, according
   to Hutchinson?
2. What percentage of the population uses illegal drugs, as
   stated by the author?
3. What is the real agenda of those who advocate the use of
   marijuana for medical purposes, in Hutchinson's
   opinion?

Asa Hutchinson, speech to Baylor University, Waco, Texas, September 16, 2002.

In many circles today, U.S. drug policy is under attack. It's being criticized by those primarily who favor some type of a legalization agenda, but it's also being challenged by those who say Europe's got a good idea, where they decriminalize drugs or they move toward harm reduction. Harm reduction is where you try to diminish the harm that comes from illegal drug use. Some European cities actually distribute needles to facilitate drug use. They have "injection rooms" in some parts of Europe to facilitate the individual's injection of illegal drugs, to get them off the street. In some ways, that reduces the harm that might come to them because they're off the street. It also reduces the impact on society because you don't see that.

But that's the European model. I think it sells people short, sells hope short. But that is being argued that that's the direction we should go in the United States. . . .

Drug War Myths

This agenda of legalization is perpetuated, in my judgment, by four or five myths that have been promoted by those who seek to change our current policy and myths that are believed by some because they have lost hope. I want to examine some of these myths for a few moments tonight.

The first myth is there has been no progress in our fight against drugs. Sometimes you hear it expressed in a little bit harsher tones, that the drug war is a miserable failure. Well, former United Nations Ambassador Jeanne Kirkpatrick once said "Americans need to face the truth about themselves, no matter how pleasant it is." And so we face the truth about ourselves, we find that there is some pleasant news.

First, on the demand side, we've reduced casual use, chronic use, and prevented others from even starting. Overall drug use in the United States is down by half since the late 1970s. That's nine and a half million people fewer using drugs today on a regular basis than 20 years ago. When it comes to cocaine use, we've reduced cocaine use by an astounding 70 percent during the last 15 years. That's over four million people fewer using cocaine on a regular basis today than 15 years ago. Those numbers represent real lives. Those are people in our families, our neighborhoods, and our communities.

Perseverance

And you know, if we achieved that kind of success on any other social problem, from domestic violence to child abuse, someone would receive the Medal of Freedom because they did such a good job. But somehow, we judge our progress against this social problem of drugs by a different standard, and we've bought into the idea of where is the victory, where is the win, when in fact you have to have perseverance. Because as long as you have depression in society, as long as you have greed and, quite frankly, as long as you have teenagers, you're going to have a battle with illegal substances. And so every generation has to face this, and we have to persevere.

Because we've made progress doesn't mean that we should all clap our hands and say the battle is over. We have still much·progress to make. We're concerned with emerging drug treats like Ecstasy—80 percent of which comes from the Netherlands, by the way; and methamphetamine, some of which is manufactured in our back yard. The fact is that our current policy, balancing prevention, enforcement of our laws, with treatment, have kept drug usage outside the scope of acceptable behavior in the United States.

To put it in perspective, less than 5 percent of the population uses illegal drugs of any kind. That's less than 16 million users of all forms of illegal drugs. Contrast that to the fact that on tobacco there are 66 million users, and with alcohol there are 109 million users. And so it is 16 million on illegal drugs, 109 million alcohol users. And so that, to me, is a successful policy when you have less than 5 percent of the population using illegal drugs of any form.

Drug policy also has an impact on general crime. A European study found violent crime and property crime increased in the late 1990s in every wealthy country except the United States. And I think our effective drug policy had something to do with that.

European Models

If you look at the European model of decriminalization that I mentioned, I think that there are some signals that it is not turning out the way they hoped.

In the Netherlands, you can actually go on a drug vaca-

tion, where you can go into Amsterdam, you can go into a
. . . coffee shop, you can buy all kinds of marijuana and it is
legal. But if you go into the red light district, which I did
with the chief of police, a law enforcement officer, a DEA
[Drug Enforcement Administration] agent, and it is so open
in terms of drug use that people came up to our group with
law enforcement presence and said, "Do you want to buy
Ecstasy? Do you want to buy methamphetamine? Do you
want to buy heroin?"

Drug Control Works

The easy cynicism that has grown up around the drug issue
is no accident. Sowing it has been the deliberate aim of a
decades-long campaign by proponents of legalization, critics
whose mantra is "nothing works," and whose central insight
appears to be that they can avoid having to propose the un-
mentionable—a world where drugs are ubiquitous and
where use and addiction would skyrocket—if they can hide
behind the bland management critique that drug control efforts are "unworkable."

Yet recent history shows otherwise. During the late 1980s
and early 1990s, an engaged government and citizenry took
on the drug issue and forced down drug use, with declines
observed among 12th graders in every year between 1985
and 1992. The Federal Government supplied leadership, but
so did parents and clergy, media and community groups, and
state and local leaders.

The good news is that, in many cases, what worked then can
work now. To make up the ground we have lost, we need
only to recover the lessons of that recent past. We know that
when we push against the drug problem it recedes. We will
push against the drug problem; it will recede.

Office of Drug Control Policy, *2002 National Drug Control Strategy*, 2002.

And so legalization in part led to an open policy in many
arenas of drugs in that country. As a result, the Dutch are
thinking about reversing some of the direction of the liberal
approach of the last few years.

And so we have had success, and the European direction I
don't think is the right way to go.

The DEA, though, is involved in the enforcement side.
We enforce our laws. We go after the drug trafficking orga-

nizations. And some of you might say, well, we're really not having any success in putting the traffickers out of business. Well, let's examine this for just a moment.

First of all, our responsibility is to increase the risk to the traffickers and, to the extent that we can, to reduce the availability of drugs on the street. I think we have had some success. Since [the September 11, 2001, terrorist attacks] a year ago now—we've had an increase of law enforcement presence on the border and in the airports. The result has been an increase in drug seizures.

Customs officials seized more than 16,000 pounds of cocaine along the border in the last six months, almost twice as much as the same period in the last year. In McAllen, Texas, seizures of methamphetamine are up 425 percent. In Laredo, heroin seizures are up 172 percent. Enforcement makes a difference, along the border and in the airports. And the costs and the risks to traffickers go up. . . .

We have reduced the cocaine that comes in the United States by 100 metric tons over the last five years. So don't let anyone tell you we have not had success in our fight against drugs. The failure argument is simply nonsense. There is success.

The Second Myth

The second myth that they always try to perpetuate is that somehow we're always locking up the users and our prisons are filled with those that are simple users and possessors of drugs. Have you ever heard that? Well, let's look at the real facts.

In federal prison, if you look at all the drug cases in federal prison, 95 percent of the drug cases are for trafficking offenses. And the 5 percent that are for drug offenses are usually those that are plea bargained down or they're convicted of multiple offenses. In federal prison, clearly, they are for trafficking. In my experience as a federal prosecutor, you have to work very hard in the United States to get to jail for simply using illegal drugs.

Now, that doesn't mean there shouldn't be accountability. If you're arrested for possession of marijuana, you ought to go to court, you pay a fine, there's accountability. It's a criminal record that will go with you for a lifetime. There's a consequence to illegal drug use. But the fact is, we are not locking up and sending to prison those people who are convicted of simple possession of drugs.

The Michigan Department of Corrections just completed a study of their inmate population. Let me tell you what they found in the state of Michigan. They found that the state had a total inmate population of 47,000. Out of that, 500 were incarcerated on simple drug possession charges. Only 500 out of 47,000. And of those, most of those, again, had been charged with multiple offenses, or pled down. A very, very small percent ever go to jail for possession offenses. And so it is nonsense, that "our jails are filled with casual users."

The Myth About Marijuana

The third myth that has been perpetuated in society today is that marijuana is not harmful. Well, young people need to be told the honest risks, because risks, and the understanding of those risks, discourage use. And the fact is that 225,000 Americans seek treatment each year because of marijuana addiction. More teens are in treatment for marijuana addiction than any other illegal drug, including alcohol.

Why do they go to treatment for marijuana? It's because it is a harmful substance that has an addiction capability in which they see a need in their own life for treatment. Marijuana is harmful in and of itself, but also it, in some instances, leads to other drug use.

Dr. Fletcher Brothers runs a Freedom Village, a faith-based organization that is the largest privately owned home for troubled teenagers in the country. And Dr. Brothers has been doing that for three decades. He's seen a lot of teens mess up their lives. And this is what he had to say about marijuana: "Never once, after dealing with thousands and thousands of addicts, have I ever dealt with a heroin addict, a cocaine addict, or anybody else that didn't start with marijuana."

Marijuana is harmful in and of itself, but it is a start of a lifetime of drug problems in some instances.

I know that some of you are thinking, well, how about medical marijuana? Well, let me just caution you to think clearly about this. How do we in our society determine what is good medicine and bad medicine? We have a rigorous approval process that is peer reviewed, that is determined by the scientific and medical community. Does the American Medical Association say that smoking marijuana has a medical benefit and doctors ought to prescribe to a sick patient smoking marijuana? The American Medical Association does not say that. They have supported continued regulation and prohibition on smoking marijuana. They do not recognize it as any medical benefit. And the same thing is true for the federal Food and Drug Administration. Whenever you talk about marijuana, we have to go through that same scientific medical review process, and we listen to them.

Now, there is some medical benefit to an active ingredient in marijuana, and that active ingredient is synthesized into Marinol, and it is actually prescribed by doctors. If there's any need, a doctor can prescribe it in pill form, called Marinol. But that's not enough for those people in some states who say, we want to smoke our marijuana. And that's simply the motivation. It is a legalization argument that they're making, and they're using the cloak of medical marijuana to get to their real agenda of legalization.

Treatment

The fourth myth is that there's not any new ideas in our fight against drugs. I'm pleased to say that there are a lot of new ideas out there that are working. One of them is what I believe is a very effective treatment program for nonviolent individuals who have an addiction problem and a crime problem. And that is called drug treatment courts, where you can go instead of going into prison when you have an addiction problem. You go into a treatment program with accountability—where you have drug testing, you have to go through a rigorous treatment program, reporting to the court. And if you don't move successfully through that program, you can have the threat of going to jail.

That has resulted in a 70 percent success rate. And this is a new idea that is expanding. We have drug treatment courts in Texas. They need to be expanded. President [George W.] Bush has invested in these. But I've gone across the nation

23

talking about drug treatment courts and how they're successful. They make a difference in the lives of individuals.

Jennifer Malloy, in Youngstown, Ohio, was a graduate of a drug treatment court. I was there in the courtroom. I listened to her story. And she was crack addict. She had a college degree, she was a professional, but she got addicted. And when she did that, she started committing crimes in order to support her addiction. She went into voluntary treatment programs. Voluntary treatment programs did not work. Her family intervened with her, and that did not work. Finally, she was arrested. And sitting in jail she knew, finally came face-to-face with the fact, that she needed treatment. She goes into the drug court program. And there, for a year, she went through this rigorous program and graduated. She was restored to her family. She has a job. And on her graduation day, she had her charges dismissed. And she looked to the judge and said, "I want to hug you." And she hugged the judge. And then she turned to her arresting officer and said, "Thank you for saving my life."

I tell that story because it connects what we do in law enforcement with the other side of what we're trying to do in the anti-drug arena. And that is to increase the treatment of individuals to get over addiction problems. They tie together. They're not in opposition to each other.

We Must Not Surrender

How do we win this battle? Well, it's simple—simple, but it's long and it takes a lot of perseverance. You win by not retreating. Victory can only be achieved one life at a time. That means there are new lives to be influenced every day, and that's one of the greatest rewards of public service.

Americans should never forget the story of Lt. Col. William Barrett Travis and the Alamo. On February 24, 1836, when he and his men were at the Alamo under attack, he wrote this letter: "To the people of Texas and all Americans in the world. I am besieged by Santa Ana and his forces. The enemy has demanded a surrender. Otherwise, we are to be put to the sword. I have answered the demand with a cannon shot. I shall never surrender or retreat."

And then he said this: "I call upon you, in the name of liberty, patriotism, and everything dear to the American character, to come to our aid."

Ladies and gentlemen, in fighting against drugs in our country, it is my view that we should not surrender. We should not give in. . . . Doing so would be giving up an opportunity for success, of making our country better, stronger, and freer. And in doing so, I believe that we'll strengthen that American character that was so important in 1836, that American character that is so important today, and that American character that will be so important to the next generation of America.

"Putting people in prison has not ended the illegal use of drugs."

The War on Drugs Has Failed

Matthew B. Stannard

In the following viewpoint, Matthew B. Stannard argues that the war on drugs is a failure. More Americans are using illegal drugs than ever before, and as a result, more people are arrested and imprisoned for illegal drug use than any other crime. Stannard contends that the solution to illegal drug use is not to imprison drug users but to provide treatment for them. Stannard, a former reporter for the *Oakland Tribune*, now writes for the *San Francisco Chronicle*.

As you read, consider the following questions:
1. According to the author, how many people are incarcerated in U.S. prisons?
2. What newly popular drug have more users taken up despite the war on drugs, according to Stannard?
3. According to Joseph McNamara, why is the government's National Strategy for Drug Control a failure?

[In 1989] then-President George Bush hoisted a bag of crack cocaine for the cameras and proclaimed that "the gravest domestic threat facing our nation today is drugs."

Expanding upon his predecessors' tough policies, Bush launched the most ambitious and expensive battle ever against narcotics and drug peddlers, setting nine goals for the nation to meet within a decade.

With opinion polls showing overwhelming public support, Bush and Congress endowed law enforcement with awesome powers for waging an all-out war against drugs—unprecedented legislative and legal authority, a new government agency with more than 100 drug-battling agents, and a budget $53 billion larger than any before proposed.

But despite all the fanfare and huge investment in the artillery against drugs, the war failed. Ten years and more than $100 billion later, only two of Bush's goals have been met.

The Drug War Has Failed

More youths are doing dope today, and more people are ending up in medical emergency rooms with overdoses and drug-related problems. Meanwhile, the amount of drugs used nationwide has remained virtually the same.

The tough law enforcement policies have succeeded mainly in packing the nation's prisons with drug users and drug law breakers, leaving the United States with more people in prison than any other country, and swelling the prison population to 1.8 million, larger than all but three of the nation's cities. Only one in 10 of those prisoners receives drug treatment; many are released with the same drug problems and soon return to a life of crime.

Faced with that evidence, law enforcement officials and drug war hawks like former Attorney General Edwin Meese are beginning to meet therapists and drug war doves like the Hoover Institution's Joseph McNamara halfway. What is emerging is a new approach that combines the strengths of criminal justice with substance abuse treatment.

"I hate to sound like a bleeding-heart liberal, but you need to attack it from two different ways. Enforcement alone does not work," said one veteran Oakland narcotics officer. "Just tossing people in prison is not the answer."

Drug Use Continues Unabated

Putting people in prison has not ended the illegal use of drugs. Since 1971, the annual National Household Survey on Drug Abuse has asked thousands of Americans whether they used illegal drugs in the past 12 months. The percentage answering "Yes" has not changed significantly since before Bush's 1989 speech from the White House Oval Office.

Cocaine—the scourge of the 1980's, by popular belief, though it actually has fallen out of favor since President Ronald Reagan's administration—continued its decline after Bush's speech. But old favorites like heroin and marijuana have held strong, and increasing numbers of users have taken up newly popular drugs like today's stronger methamphetamine.

Young people, in particular, have been turning on to drugs in numbers that only in 1999 began to decline. Bush's 10-year plan called for the number of adolescent Americans using drugs to be cut in half within a decade. Instead it increased by more than 20 percent, as young people grew more tolerant of drug use, continued to smoke marijuana and discovered more potent forms of heroin.

Prison as a Growth Industry

Where the war did have an impact was on the nation's prison population. Police, prosecutors, politicians and the public got fed up with criminals in the 1980s—and especially with drug offenders. So they put them in prison, in larger numbers and for longer sentences than ever before.

"If you take California, the statistics are kind of stunning," said Franklin Zimring, director of the Earl Warren Legal Institute at the Boalt Hall School of Law at the University of California, Berkeley.

"There were more people in 1991 in California prisons for drug offenses than were in California prisons for all offenses in 1980. Not only did the number of drug offenders go up fifteen-fold, but that one unit of the California prison population was larger than the whole prison population had been a decade before," he said.

"You can't find too many historical episodes like that in American history."

The same thing happened nationwide. More people are now arrested for breaking drug laws than for driving under the influence, theft, simple assault or any other crime. Statistics show that once in the system, drug offenders are more likely to be convicted and receive longer sentences than any other nonviolent offenders in both state and federal courts.

Between 1985 and 1998, under a deluge of drug criminals, the nation's prison population expanded from 744,206 to 1.8 million.

When the prisons were filled, the taxpayers built more. In 1980 the total nationwide operating budget for state and federal prisons and jails was $7 billion. By 1998, it was $39 billion. California spends more on prisons than any other state—about $4.6 billion per year.

One Benefit

Locking up 1.8 million drug violators and other criminals has at least one clear benefit, some experts say. The nation's crime rate has plummeted since Bush's speech: by one major measure, the National Crime Victimization Survey, crime hasn't been this low since 1973.

"The criminal justice system can take primary credit for this," said Morgan Reynolds, director of the criminal justice center at the private National Center for Policy Analysis and a longtime supporter of incarceration as a tool against crime.

"That's gotten a lot more respect lately," he said. "More police, new police tactics including community policing, tougher laws, and of course the fact that we have more offenders out of commission behind bars."

Treatment Is Missing

But others worry about what happens to those offenders once they are behind bars—or, more accurately, what doesn't happen: treatment for their drug problems.

Steven Belenko, a researcher with the National Center on Addiction and Substance Abuse at Columbia University in New York City, reports that a majority of both state and federal prisoners had links to illicit drug use.

About 19 percent of state prisoners and 55 percent of federal prisoners had been convicted of a drug law offense, he

Ten-Year Goals

Section 1005 of the Anti-Drug Abuse Act of 1988 requires that each National Drug Control Strategy include "comprehensive, research-based, long-range goals for reducing drug abuse in the United States." The first National Drug Control Strategy was unveiled on September 5, 1989, with the following 10-year goals:

GOAL	OUTCOME
1 A 50-percent reduction in the number of people reporting any illegal use of drugs in the past month. **FAILED**	In 1988, 7.7 percent of all Americans aged 12 or older reported using an illicit drug in the past 30 days. In 1998, that percentage was 6.2 percent, a 19 percent decrease.
2 A 50-percent reduction in the number of adolescents reporting any illegal use of drugs in the past month. **FAILED**	In 1988, 8.1 percent of 12–17 year olds reported using an illicit drug in the past 30 days. In 1998, that percentage was 9.9 percent, a 22 percent increase.
3 A 50-percent reduction in the number of people reporting less often than once-a-month cocaine use in the past year. **SUCCEEDED**	In 1988, the percentage of people who reported using cocaine on less than 12 days in the past year was 2.6 percent. By 1998, the percentage was 1.1 percent.
4 A 50-percent reduction in the number of people reporting weekly or more frequent cocaine use. **SUCCEEDED**	In 1988, the percentage of people who reported using cocaine on 51 or more days in the past year was 0.6 percent. In 1998, the percentage was 0.3 percent, a 50 percent decrease.
5 A 50-percent reduction in the number of adolescents reporting past month cocaine use. **FAILED**	In 1988, 1.2 percent of all 12–17 year olds reported using cocaine in the past month. By 1998, that percentage was 0.8 percent, a 33 percent decrease.
6 A 50-percent reduction in the number of hospital emergency room mentions for cocaine, marijuana, heroin, and dangerous drugs. **FAILED**	In 1990, 635,480 emergency room drug mentions were recorded in the United States. In 1997, officials recorded 943,937, a 48 percent increase.

GOAL	OUTCOME

7a A 50-percent reduction in estimated amounts of cocaine, marijuana, heroin, and dangerous drugs entering the United States. **UNCERTAIN**

There are no reliable estimates of drugs entering the United States. However, in 1988, an ounce of pure cocaine cost $3,374; an ounce of pure heroin cost $51,200. In 1997, those ounces cost $2,807 and $33,453, respectively. Many experts believe that decreases in price indicate an increase in supply.

7b A 50-percent reduction in the number of people reporting that cocaine, marijuana, heroin, and dangerous drugs are easy to obtain in their communities. **FAILED**

In 1991, 62.1 percent of surveyed adults rated marijuana fairly easy or very easy to obtain. 43.7 percent said the same about cocaine, and 28.3 percent said the same about heroin. In 1998, those percentages had changed to 58.2 percent, 38.3 percent, and 28.3 percent, respectively.

8 A 50-percent decrease in domestic marijuana production. **UNCERTAIN**

There are no reliable estimates of marijuana production in the United States. However, the street price of marijuana fell sharply between 1988 and 1997, from about $215 per ounce to about $149. Many experts believe that decreases in price indicate an increase in supply.

9 A 50-percent reduction in the number of high school students who report that they do not disapprove of illegal drug use. **FAILED**

In 1989, 89.8 percent of surveyed 12th graders disapproved of people who smoked marijuana regularly, 96.4 percent of people who used LSD regularly, 96.4 percent of people who used cocaine regularly, and 97.5 percent of people who used heroin regularly. In 1998, those percentages had declined to 81.2 percent for marijuana, 93.5 percent for LSD, 95.6 for cocaine, and 96.6 for heroin.

Sources: National Household Survey on Drug Abuse, Monitoring the Future Study, United States Department of Justice, Office of National Drug Control Policy, Substance Abuse and Mental Health Services Administration.

said. Seventeen percent of state prisoners and 10 percent of all federal prisoners had committed a crime to get money to buy drugs. Thirty percent of state inmates and 16 percent of federal inmates were under the influence of drugs or drugs combined with alcohol when they committed their crime. And 64 percent of state inmates and 43 percent of federal inmates had used drugs regularly—most of them in the month prior to their arrest.

Number of Arrests, by Type of Drug Law Violations, 1982–2002

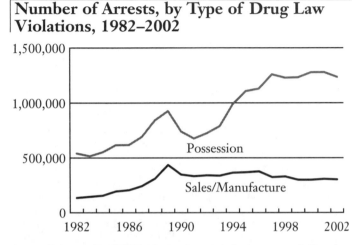

According to the UCR, drug abuse violations are defined as state and/or local offenses relating to the unlawful possession, sale, use, growing, manufacturing, and making of narcotic drugs including opium or cocaine and their derivatives, marijuana, synthetic narcotics, and dangerous nonnarcotic drugs such as barbiturates.

More than four-fifths of drug law violation arrests are for possession.

FBI, Uniform Crime Reports, 2002.

"If you measure that against the amount of substance abuse treatment and prevention activities that take place in prison, it's quite a dramatic figure, because only about 10 to 15 percent of inmates are getting any kind of substance abuse treatment when they're in custody," he said. "So there's a huge gap."

And it's getting wider.

According to the U.S. Department of Justice, more state prisoners admitted using drugs before their arrest in 1991 than 1997, but fewer got to participate in prison drug treatment programs each year.

By 1997, more than eight out of 10 state prisoners said they had used drugs, but only one in 10 received prison drug treatment. And slightly more than half of those received treatment in a residential facility, the kind of treatment experts say stands the best chance of preventing a return to drug abuse and crime.

Saving Taxpayers' Money

Residential treatment is expensive—about $6,500 per inmate per year, Belenko estimated, including vocational training and follow-up care. But each inmate who stays clean for a year after release saves taxpayers $68,800 through wages, savings in health care and prison costs, and reduced crime, he said.

"With these huge numbers of inmates now who are getting released, if they're released untreated, it's likely—given past research—that without intervention a large portion of them will return to using drugs and committing crimes related to those drug problems," he said.

Belenko's report is getting attention. California is one of several states experimenting with increased drug treatment in the correctional system and expanded after-care for ex-felons. And Belenko's ideas are echoed by longtime drug war hawks like Reynolds and Meese, and in proposals from [former] Drug Czar Barry McCaffrey.

"It is clear that we cannot arrest our way out of the problem of chronic drug abuse and drug-driven crime," McCaffrey said in a recent speech. "We cannot continue to apply policies and programs that do not deal with the root causes of substance abuse and attendant crime."

Interdiction vs. Treatment

Some treatment advocates and drug war critics say the new drug warriors are not putting their money where their mouth is yet.

On July 22, 1999, for example, McCaffrey announced his

support for new regulations improving the quality and accessibility of methadone treatment for heroin addicts. But a day later, he called for a $1 billion expansion of the United States' longstanding military interdiction efforts in the jungles of Colombia.

McCaffrey has been speaking in favor of a less punitive drug war "practically since he came in three years ago, and there has been almost no change in the budget," said attorney Eric Sterling, president of the Criminal Justice Policy Foundation in Washington. "Where is the evidence he's put any effort into fighting for more treatment?"

The Clinton administration's drug enforcement budget request for [2000] is $17.8 billion.

About 66 percent of that budget is earmarked for controlling the supply of illicit drugs through domestic and international law enforcement. The rest—about 34 percent—is divided between treatment, prevention, and research.

Many critics of the nation's drug policy believe those percentages should be reversed.

"I think we'll be living in a better country if we have a lot of drug treatment in prison," Zimring said. "(But) we're too busy expanding penal facilities to provide any content other than incarceration in them."

Other policymakers and observers say the changes may be out of [Bill] Clinton and McCaffrey's hands, because there is little political will in Congress to change the drug budget's ratio of law enforcement to treatment.

"I don't get punished (politically) if I vote against money for treatment. But I do get punished if I vote against more money for the law enforcement aspects," said Dr. Herbert Kleber, deputy for demand reduction in the National Drug Policy Office from 1989 until 1991. "Most congressmen want to get reelected. Why are they going to vote against their own self interests?"

Changing the Goals

Ten years from now, the success or failure of the new war on drugs will be measured in terms similar to the old one's. Although the National Strategy for Drug Control has been rewritten each year since Bush first announced it in 1989, each has included a set of short-term and long-term goals.

Clinton's most recent strategy includes a total of 97 goals, with 12 key objectives, compared with the Bush administration's original nine. Some of those objectives—reducing the availability of illicit drugs by 50 percent, halving drug use by youth, cutting overall drug use by 50 percent—are identical to goals in Bush's plan. The deadline to meet them is 2007.

"Every one of the indications that they themselves had set years ago are not working . . . then McCaffrey has the chutz-pah to say, 'You can't judge us now, you have to wait 10 years,'" said Joseph McNamara, former San Jose police chief and now a sharp critic of anti-drug policy at the Hoover Institution at Stanford University. "They just keep changing the goals. Every time they fail, they just gloss over that."

"Since the Reagan administration made illegal drug use a high national priority, drug abuse in the United States has decreased significantly."

The War on Drugs Has Reduced the Demand for Illegal Drugs

Edmund F. McGarrell

The war on drugs has reduced illegal drug use in the United States, contends Edmund F. McGarrell in the following viewpoint. The number of Americans using cocaine and marijuana declined significantly during the 1980s and remained at low levels during the 1990s, he claims. Legalizing these drugs would have disastrous consequences, McGarrell argues; more than 80 percent of high school seniors have used alcohol—a controlled but legal substance—while only 10 percent have tried cocaine and heroin, both illegal drugs. If these drugs were legalized, he believes, many teens would be tempted to try them, and drug usage would soar. McGarrell is the director of the Crime Control Policy Center at the Hudson Institute, a policy research organization.

As you read, consider the following questions:
1. According to the author, by what percentage has the number of marijuana and cocaine users been reduced since the Reagan administration?
2. How many new marijuana users were there in 1975 compared to 1996, as cited by McGarrell?
3. To what event does McGarrell attribute an increase in teen use of marijuana?

New Mexico Governor Gary Johnson has generated controversy lately by advocating the legalization of various narcotic drugs. Johnson has joined former Baltimore Mayor Curt Schmoke and journalists such as William F. Buckley Jr. in calling for decriminalization and attempting to place the issue on the public-policy agenda.

Although there are several premises on which most advocates of drug legalization rely, one of the most common themes is that America has lost the war on drugs. This has become something of a mantra among legalizers, yet they have offered little evidence on whether the war really has been lost. In fact, there is evidence both that drug laws work and that legalization would constitute a declaration of unconditional surrender by public-policy analysts who seek to minimize use of harmful drugs.

Drug Abuse Has Declined

As Figure 1 illustrates, since the Reagan administration made illegal drug use a high national priority, drug abuse in the

Figure 1. Trends in Current Drug Use

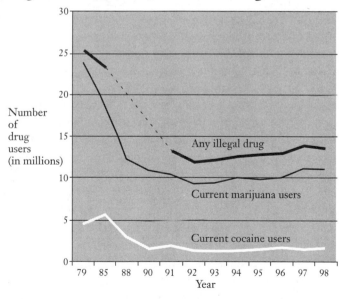

National Household Survey, 1998.

Figure 2. Trends in Drug Use Among U.S. Twelfth-Graders

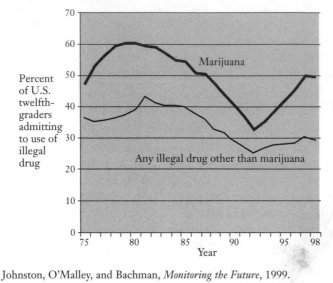

Percent of U.S. twelfth-graders admitting to use of illegal drug

Marijuana

Any illegal drug other than marijuana

Year

Johnston, O'Malley, and Bachman, *Monitoring the Future*, 1999.

United States has decreased significantly. The number of current marijuana and cocaine users has been reduced by 46 and 68 percent, respectively. In absolute numbers, this translates into 11.8 million fewer drug users overall, including 8.5 million fewer marijuana users and 3.9 million fewer cocaine users. Figure 2 indicates similar trends among high-school seniors. There have also been dramatic declines in the rates of new marijuana and cocaine users. Whereas during 1975 there were approximately 3.5 million new marijuana users, in 1996 there were less than half as many. The decline in the number of new cocaine users has been even steeper. For all the elite's ridicule of [former first lady] Nancy Reagan's "Just Say No" campaign, the data suggest that many Americans followed her advice. The declines evident during the Reagan and Bush eras have not continued during the 1990s, but neither have they escalated to pre-Reagan levels.

Teen use of various substances further suggests the likely effects of legalization. Governor Johnson states that "legalization will allow governments to regulate, tax, and control drugs." In other words, cocaine, heroin, methamphetamine,

Figure 3. Use of Legal and Illegal Drugs by U.S. Twelfth-Graders

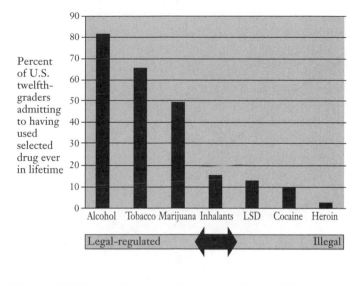

Johnston, O'Malley, and Bachman, *Monitoring the Future*, 1999.

and other illegal substances should be controlled in the same manner as tobacco and alcohol. Figure 3 suggests the potentially disastrous consequences of such a policy. As the graph indicates, over 80 percent of all U.S. high-school seniors have used "legal but controlled" alcohol, and two-thirds have used tobacco. Just 12 percent of seniors have used the illegal substance LSD, and less than 10 percent have sampled the illegal substances of cocaine and heroin. For marijuana, a substance that has an active lobby for legalization and where possession has largely been de facto decriminalized by many big-city police departments, the number of users is significantly higher than for substances that are more clearly illegal. Thus the trends indicate that real legalization of these drugs is likely to generate rates of cocaine and heroin use closer to today's teen use of alcohol and tobacco.

Research on illegal drug use among teens has found a well-established negative relationship between perceptions of the harmfulness of use and actual use. Just as teen marijuana use increased when President [Bill] Clinton's "I never inhaled" statement[1] became a national joke (see Figure 2), it is predictable that endorsement of the decriminalization position, let alone actual decriminalization itself, will send a message to the young that drug use is not that harmful. Use will undoubtedly increase. Governor Johnson has stated, "I have no doubt that drugs will be legalized in this country. No doubt." We can only hope that he is wrong.

1. When President Bill Clinton was asked whether or not he had ever used illegal drugs, he made this reply, attempting to head off negative judgments of his behavior.

"Law enforcement has been unable to seriously disrupt either the supply of or the demand for illegal drugs."

The Demand for Illegal Drugs Remains Strong

Timothy Lynch

Timothy Lynch argues in the following viewpoint that the American public is increasingly dissatisfied with the war on drugs. Despite government claims that the war on drugs is reducing demand for illegal drugs and disrupting supply, illegal drug use remains strong, he maintains. According to Lynch, billions of tax dollars are spent every year in a fruitless attempt to keep drugs from entering the country. As long as people want to use illegal drugs, the government is helpless to change the laws of supply and demand, he contends. Lynch is the director of the Cato Institute's Project on Criminal Justice.

As you read, consider the following questions:
1. Which states have approved the legalization of marijuana for medical purposes, according to Lynch?
2. Why is drug use wrong, according to supporters of the drug war?
3. What does William Bennett compare drug legalization to, according to Lynch?

Timothy Lynch, "War No More: The Folly and Futility of Drug Probation," *National Review*, vol. 53, February 5, 2001. Copyright © 2000 by the Cato Institute. All rights reserved. Reproduced by permission.

America's drug policies are never seriously debated in Washington. Year after year, our elected representatives focus on two questions: How much more money should we spend on the drug war? and, How should it be spent? In the months preceding elections, politicians typically try to pin blame for the drug problem on one another. After the election, the cycle begins anew.

Outside the capital, however, there is growing unease about the war on drugs. More and more Americans are concluding that the drug war has been given a chance to work—and has failed. Voters in California, Arizona, Oregon, Washington, Nevada, Alaska, and Maine have rejected the lobbying efforts of federal officials and approved initiatives calling for the legalization of marijuana for medicinal purposes. Two sitting governors, Jesse Ventura of Minnesota and Gary Johnson of New Mexico, have declared the drug war a failure. As public opinion continues to turn against the war, we can expect more elected officials to speak out.

Federal officials do not yet appreciate the extent of public dissatisfaction with the war on drugs. Congress continues to propose and enact laws with such platitudinous titles as "The Drug-Free Century Act." Not many people outside the capital are even paying attention to those laws, and even fewer take the rhetoric seriously.

The Drug-Reform Movement

To be sure, some people of good will continue to support the drug war. Their rationale is that we may not be close to achieving a "drug-free" society, but our present situation would only deteriorate if the government were to stop prosecuting the drug war. The burden of persuasion on that proposition has always rested with drug reformers. But nowadays it is a burden reformers happily accept, buoyed as they are by the realization that momentum in the debate is shifting in their direction.

Reformers are as eager as ever to debate the efficacy of the drug laws—while supporters of the drug war discuss the issue only grudgingly. Reformers ask: Why should an adult man or woman be arrested, prosecuted, and imprisoned for using heroin, opium, cocaine, or marijuana? The answer, according to the most prominent supporters of the drug war, is simple: Drug use is wrong. It is wrong because it is immoral, and it is immoral because it degrades human beings. The prominent social scientist James Q. Wilson has articulated that view as follows: "Even now, when the dangers of drug use are well understood, many educated people still discuss the drug problem in almost every way except the right way. They talk about the 'costs' of drug use and the 'socioeconomic factors' that shape that use. They rarely speak plainly—drug use is wrong because it is immoral and it is immoral because it enslaves the mind and destroys the soul."

William J. Bennett, America's first drug czar, has expressed a similar view: "A citizen in a drug-induced haze, whether on his backyard deck or on a mattress in a ghetto crack house, is not what the Founding Fathers meant by the 'pursuit of happiness.'. . . Helpless wrecks in treatment centers, men chained by their noses to cocaine—these people are slaves."

The Government's Role

Wilson, Bennett, and their supporters believe that to eradicate this form of slavery, the government should vigorously investigate, prosecute, and jail anyone who sells, uses, or possesses mind-altering drugs. The criminal sanction should be used—in Bennett's words—"to take drug users off the streets and deter new users from becoming more deeply involved in so hazardous an activity."

For more than 25 years, the political establishment has offered unflagging support for the ban on drugs. In 1973, President [Richard] Nixon created the Drug Enforcement Administration, a police agency that focuses exclusively on federal drug-law violations. President [Ronald] Reagan designated narcotics an official threat to America's national security; he also signed legislation authorizing the military to assist federal and state police agencies in the drug war. In 1988, Congress created the Office of National Drug Control Policy; President [George] Bush appointed Bennett national drug czar to centralize control and coordinate activities of federal agencies in the drug war. President [Bill] Clinton appointed a former military commander, Gen. Barry McCaffrey, as drug czar.

Since the early 1970s, Congress has been escalating the

federal government's drug-war efforts. In 1979, the federal government spent $900 million on various antidrug programs; in 1989, it spent $5 billion; by 1999, it was spending nearly $18 billion.

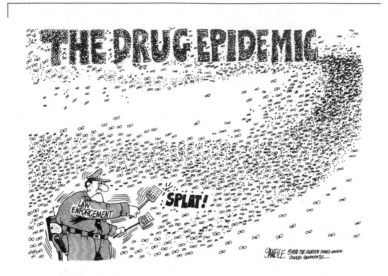

Gamble. © 1986 by The Florida Times–Union Cowles Syndicate. Reprinted by permission of Ed Gamble.

According to the Office of National Drug Control Policy, vigorous law-enforcement tactics help reduce drug abuse chiefly by reducing demand and disrupting supply. Enforcement of the drug laws reduces demand by increasing social disapproval of substance abuse; arrest and threatened imprisonment also offer a powerful incentive for addicts to take treatment seriously. Drug enforcement disrupts supply by detecting and dismantling drug rings, which facilitate the movement of drugs from suppliers to the streets.

Results from the War on Drugs

Congress has devoted billions of dollars to these tasks, and there have been palpable results. To begin with, the criminal-justice system has grown much larger: There are more police officers, prosecutors, judges, and prison guards than ever before. The number of arrests, convictions, and prisoners has increased exponentially; so has the amount of seized contraband. In February 1999, the *New York Times* reported that "every 20 seconds, someone in America is arrested for a drug violation. Every week, on average, a new jail or prison is built to lock up more people in the world's largest penal system."

There is certainly a lot of government activity; but is the Office of National Drug Control Policy really achieving its twin objectives of reducing demand and disrupting supply? The demand for illegal drugs remains strong. According to the National Household Survey on Drug Abuse, 11 million Americans can be classified as "current users" (past month) of marijuana and 1.75 million Americans as current users of cocaine. As startling as those numbers are, they represent only the tip of the proverbial iceberg. Millions of other individuals can be classified as "occasional users," and tens of thousands of people use less popular illicit drugs, such as heroin and methamphetamine. In short: The government's own statistics admit that millions and millions of Americans break the law every single month.

The supply of drugs has not been hampered in any serious way by the war on drugs. A commission on federal law-enforcement practices chaired by former FBI director William Webster recently offered this blunt assessment of the interdiction efforts: "Despite a record number of seizures and a flood of legislation, the Commission is not aware of any evidence that the flow of narcotics into the United States has been reduced." Perhaps the most dramatic evidence of the failure of the drug war is the flourishing of open-air drug markets in Washington, D.C.—the very city in which the drug czar and the Drug Enforcement Administration have their headquarters.

A Fair Appraisal of the Drug War

Even though law enforcement has been unable to seriously disrupt either the supply of or the demand for illegal drugs, many hesitate to draw the conclusion that the drug war has failed. They choose to focus on the evils of drug use, and the need to keep up the fight against it, on the grounds that even an incomplete success is better than a surrender. But a fair appraisal of the drug war must look beyond drug use itself, and take into account all of the negative repercussions of the drug war. It is undeniable that the criminalization of drug use has created an immense and sophisticated black market that generates billions of dollars for gangster organizations. The criminal proceeds are often used to finance other criminal activity. Furthermore, rival gangs use violence to usurp and defend territory for drug sales. Innocent people die in the crossfire.

Then there is the cost. Billions of taxpayer dollars are squandered every year to keep drugs from entering the country. The government cannot even keep narcotics out of its own prisons—and yet it spends millions every month trying to keep contraband from arriving by air, land, and sea.

Prosecuting the war also involves a disturbingly large number of undesirable police practices: Paramilitary raids, roadblocks, wiretaps, informants, and property seizures have all become routine because of the difficulty of detecting drug offenses. Countless innocent people have had their phones tapped and their homes and cars searched. A criminal-justice system that devotes its limited resources to drug offenders is necessarily distracted from investigating other criminal activity—such as murder, rape, and theft.

Unfortunately, the most prominent supporters of the drug war have refused to grapple with these grim consequences of their policy. Drug legalization, they retort, would undermine the moral sanction against drug use. William Bennett has actually indulged in a comparison that would equate alternative drug policies—such as decriminalization—with surrender to the Nazis: "Imagine if, in the darkest days of 1940, Winston Churchill had rallied the West by saying, 'This war looks hopeless, and besides, it will cost too much. Hitler can't be that bad. Let's surrender and see what happens.' That is essentially what we hear from the legalizers."

Perseverance vs. Bullheadedness

After decades of ceaseless police work, it is safe to say that Bennett is confusing perseverance with bullheadedness. One thoughtful analyst, Father John Clifton Marquis, recognized—as long ago as 1990—that "when law does not promote the common good, but in fact causes it to deteriorate, the law itself becomes bad and must be changed. . . . Au-

46

thentic moral leaders cannot afford the arrogant luxury of machismo, with its refusal to consider not 'winning.'"

Marquis is correct; and this is precisely why Bennett's World War II imagery is misplaced. The notion that the drug czar is somehow leading an army against an evil foe is an example of what Marquis calls "arrogant machismo." A more apt analogy would be America's 15-year experience with alcohol prohibition: Americans rejected Prohibition because experience showed the federal liquor laws to be un-enforceable and because alcohol prohibition led to gang wars and widespread corruption. The war on drugs has created a similar set of problems.

The most valuable lesson that can be drawn from the Prohibition experience is that government cannot effectively engineer social arrangements. Policymakers simply cannot repeal the economic laws of supply and demand. Nor can they foresee the unintended consequences that follow government intervention. Students of American history will someday wonder how today's lawmakers could readily admit that alcohol prohibition was a disastrous mistake, but simultaneously engage in a reckless policy of drug prohibition.

Drug policy in America needs to be reinvented, starting with a tabula rasa. Policymakers ought to address the issue in an open, honest, and mature manner. A growing number of Americans are coming to the conclusion that the law should treat substances such as marijuana and cocaine the same way it treats tobacco, beer, and whiskey: restricting sales to minors and jailing any user who endangers the safety of others (by, for example, operating an automobile while under the influence). Education, moral suasion, and noncoercive social pressure are the only appropriate ways to discourage adult drug use in a free and civil society.

> "*America's drug enforcement policies are working: from 1979 to 1994, the number of drug users in America dropped by almost half.*"

The War on Drugs Has Made Law Enforcement More Effective

Thomas A. Constantine

Thomas A. Constantine is a former superintendent of the New York State Police and former administrator for the Drug Enforcement Administration (DEA). In the following viewpoint, excerpted from his testimony before Congress in 1999, he contends that new aggressive law enforcement practices are the best way to win the war on drugs. He asserts that drug use and general crime rates have declined because of such law enforcement policies. Constantine argues against the legalization of drugs; he believes society is better off when dangerous and addictive drugs remain illegal.

As you read, consider the following questions:
1. According to Constantine, what kinds of people are behind proposals to legalize drugs?
2. By what percentage did the homicide rate decline in New York City during the 1990s, as cited by the author?
3. What are some of the tough questions that Constantine believes should be asked of drug legalization supporters?

Thomas A. Constantine, testimony before the Subcommittee on Criminal Justice, Drug Policy and Human Resources, U.S. House of Representatives, Washington, DC, July 13, 1999.

During my 39-year career in law enforcement, in my positions as Superintendent of the New York State Police and as Administrator of the Drug Enforcement Administration (DEA), and now as I return to private life, I have passionately believed that legalizing drugs is wrong, immoral, and suicidal for our society. Having seen first-hand the devastation that drug use and availability have had on many segments of our society over the past thirty years, I know deep in my heart that any effort to make more drugs available to the American people, including our children and the poor—which, make no mistake is what legalization advocates are suggesting—will have devastating consequences for our entire nation.

When I look at just who is proposing drug legalization I am struck by several things, including the fact that they are mostly affluent, well-educated and socially distant from the potential victims of their experiment. The legalization movement is well-financed and has been spawned in salons in the Upper East side of New York, country clubs on both coasts of the nation, and in locations remote from the realities of drug addiction, despair and the social decay that accompany drug use. The people who are missing from the legalization debate, and this is no accident, are mothers, religious leaders, and the loved ones of those who have been victimized by crime and addiction. Law enforcement officials are also absent from the ranks of those who are calling for legalization, not because we have a vested interest in enforcing the drug laws of the United States, but because we have seen how dangerous and divesting drug use and trafficking have been, particularly in poorer urban and rural areas of our country. . . .

The Impact of Aggressive Law Enforcement

I believe that the application of aggressive law enforcement principles and techniques, rather than drug legalization/decriminalization, is the most successful way to dismantle international drug trafficking organizations and reduce the number of drug users in this country. America's drug enforcement policies are working: from 1979 to 1994, the number of drug users in America dropped by almost half.

Aggressive law enforcement has also reduced the levels of violent crime so often associated with drug abuse and drug trafficking. Within the last several years, it has become very clear that the recent reductions in the violent crime rate within the United States in places like New York, Los Angeles and Houston—now at levels not seen since the 1960's—are due in large part to aggressive law enforcement at all levels. The New York City example is perhaps the most compelling illustration of this point. In the early 1990's, after three decades of rapidly increasing levels of violent crime, which were exacerbated by the crack epidemic, the City of New York embarked upon an ambitious program to enhance its law enforcement capabilities. City leaders increased the police department by 30%, adding 8,000 officers. Arrests for all crimes, including drug dealing, drug gang activity, and quality of life violations which had been tolerated for many years, increased by 50%. The capacity of New York prisons was also increased. The results of these actions were dramatic: the total number of homicides in 1998—633—was less than the number of murders in 1964. Over an eight-year period the number of homicides was reduced from 2262 to 633—a reduction of more than 70%.

DEA has also been aggressive in developing and implementing programs to reduce violent narcotics-related crime. One enforcement program, the Mobile Enforcement Teams (MET), lends support to local and state law enforcement agencies that are experiencing problems arising from violent drug related crime in their communities. The results of this program over the past four years indicate that aggressive law enforcement of drug laws does have a lasting impact on reducing crime and improving the quality of life for the residents of communities across the nation. Statistics indicate that on average, communities participating in the MET program have seen a 12% reduction in homicides. But just as important to me have been the scores of letters the DEA has received from leaders in these communities recognizing this decrease in crime and thanking us for helping achieve a more peaceful way of life for citizens.

Drug abuse, along with the combination of violent crime and social decay that accompany it, can be prevented. Too many people in America seem resigned to the inevitability of rampant drug use. However, effective law enforcement programs make a difference, and we must stay the course.

The Reality of Legalization

Legalization proponents are telling Americans that drugs are not dangerous, that increased addiction is not a significant threat to America, and that inner cities will be better off because it is drug dealing—not drug use—that is the problem.

The legalization advocates are not telling the truth about the consequences of their proposal. It is not that they are purposely misleading Americans, but rather they are not providing all of the information necessary for us to make a sound judgment on the issue. The logistics of legalizing drugs are overwhelming. Take pharmaceuticals for example. Despite tough regulations and strict controls, these powerful and addicting legalized drugs remain the most widely abused drugs in the country. Surely the same would happen with legalized heroin, cocaine, and methamphetamine.

The War on Drugs Has Reduced Crime

Strong drug enforcement in the United States is correlated with dramatic reductions in crime, drug use, and drug addiction rates. Historically, permissive enforcement policies brought record murder and crime rates, peak drug use levels, and increased the addict population. . . .

Tougher drug policy also reduces addiction because the criminal justice system is the number one source of treatment referrals. President [Bill] Clinton credits the justice system for saving his brother's life and many treatment centers would shut down, and addicts would die, if drug laws were repealed. In 1991, a quarter of a million inmates received their most recent drug treatment while in prison.

Robert E. Peterson, "Has the War on Drugs Reduced Crime?" www.pbs.org.

There are many tough questions to ask legalization advocates. I believe many cannot be answered adequately. Some of these include:

Will all drugs be legalized? Will we knowingly make dangerous, mind-altering, addictive substances—PCP, LSD, crack, methamphetamine—available to everyone—regardless of their health? profession? age? past criminal record?

How do we address the black market that will inevitably spring up to provide newer, purer, more potent drugs to those now addicted who cannot be satisfied with the product they obtain from the government or the private sector?

Given the fact that our record with cigarettes and alcohol is not very good, how will we limit the abundance of dangerous drugs to 18 or 21 year olds?

Who will pay for the health costs and social costs which will accrue as a result of increased drug use? Who will pay for the losses in productivity and absenteeism?

Whose taxes will pay for the thousands of babies born drug-addicted?

What responsibility will our society have to these children as they grow and have problems as a result of their drug use?

Will drug centers be located in the inner cities, or will drug distribution centers be set up in the suburbs?

And most legalization experts cannot answer this question: Can we set up a legalization pilot program in your neighborhood?

Demand Answers

These are all questions we should ask and answers we should demand. Granted, we have not yet effectively addressed all of the drug problems facing our nation today, but we must also realize that the drug issue is a very complex problem that has been with us for decades. It will take more time for us to see our way clear.

Despite this realization, it is astounding to me that legalization proponents advocate surrender. Our nation is faced with other major problems besides drug use: AIDS, declining educational standards, homelessness—yet we do not hear cries for us to abandon our efforts and surrender to inaction on these issues. Why is the drug issue different?

We do not advocate giving up on our schools, or negating everything we've done to date to find a cure for cancer—even though we have spent billions of dollars on research and we have not yet found a cure.

In closing, I ask each of you to think about these questions, and to ask yourself if we in fact would be better off as a society freely dispensing drugs to anyone who wanted them. Given the enormous challenges our nation faces in the years ahead, I cannot honestly envision a world where our surgeons, pilots, or children are given license by our government—which has an obligation to protect and defend all of us—to take dangerous and addictive drugs.

"[The war on drugs] has undermined one of the most precious cornerstones of the whole criminal justice process: the integrity of the police officer on the witness stand."

The War on Drugs Has Corrupted Law Enforcement

Joseph D. McNamara, interviewed by Michael W. Lynch

Joseph D. McNamara is the former police chief of San Jose, California, and a fellow at the Hoover Institution. In the following viewpoint, taken from an interview conducted by Michael W. Lynch, a national correspondent for *Reason* magazine, McNamara asserts that law enforcement has little effect in deterring drug use. Moreover, police methods utilizing informants and sting operations have compromised police integrity, he contends. In addition, many police officers are committing illegal searches and perjuring themselves on the witness stand because they believe such activities are justified by the necessity of winning the war on drugs.

As you read, consider the following questions:
1. What event opened McNamara's eyes about how little impact police had in the war on drugs?
2. According to McNamara, what are some of the names given to the practice of police lying on the witness stand?
3. How did the San Jose police department pay for new equipment when no money was included in the city budget, according to the author?

Michael W. Lynch, "Battlefield Conversions," *Reason*, vol. 33, January 2002, p. 36. Copyright © 2002 by the Reason Foundation, 3415 S. Sepulveda Blvd., Suite 400, Los Angeles, CA 90034, www.reason.com. Reproduced by permission.

Reason: How did you get involved in what is now called the War on Drugs?

Joseph D. McNamara: I got involved as a foot patrolman in Harlem way back in 1957. A few years later the heroin epidemic swept through Harlem and was devastating. And so the police did what the police do: We arrested everyone in sight. It soon became apparent that it wasn't reducing drug use or drug selling. My eyes were really opened one day when my partner and I arrested a heroin addict. The addicts gathered on the top floor landings of buildings, which we referred to as shooting galleries. We used to routinely bust them for possession of hypodermic needles and also for the big crime of having cookers with residues of heroin.

One day an addict asked if we could give him a break. He said, "I'll give you a pusher if you let me go." We followed him down Lenox Avenue in uniform and in a marked police car. As he talked to one man after another, it struck me how little impact the police had on the drug problem. If we hadn't known what he was talking about, we would've thought they were just two men talking sports or the weather or whatever.

A Lack of Police Integrity

Is this why police rely on informants and sting operations?

Since the police can't do their job the way they do it with other crimes, they resort to informants and to illegal searches. This is a major problem underlying police integrity throughout the United States.

[In 2001], state and local police made somewhere around 1.4 million drug arrests. Almost none of those arrests had search warrants. Sometimes the guy says, "Sure, officer, go ahead and open the trunk of my car. I have a kilo of cocaine back there but I don't want you to think I don't cooperate with the local police." Or the suspect conveniently leaves the dope on the desk or throws it at the feet of the police officer as he approaches. But often nothing like that happens.

The fact is that sometimes the officer reaches inside the suspect's pocket for the drugs and testifies that the suspect "dropped" it as the officer approached. It's so common that it's called "dropsy testimony." The lying is called "white perjury." Otherwise honest cops think it's legitimate to commit these illegal searches and to perjure themselves because they are fighting an evil. In New York it's called "testilying" and in Los Angeles it's called joining the "Liar's Club." It has lead some people to say L.A.P.D. [Los Angeles Police Department] stands for Los Angeles Perjury Department. It has undermined one of the most precious cornerstones of the whole criminal justice process: the integrity of the police officer on the witness stand.

Prohibition Leads to Corruption

As any economist can tell you, prohibition creates inherent incentives for corruption. Couple the illegality of a product with its demand and you've got a good recipe for a bad thing. The economics are simple. Because a product is illegal, the risks of getting the product to market are greater, leading directly to higher prices—nobody is going to charge spare change in a business where selling can land you in the clink for more years than committing murder. Thus, the illegality of drugs drives the prices sky-high, and it doesn't take [much] to figure out that with that much money involved, somebody—poor hoodlum, high-school dropout, white-collar exec or police officer—is going to figure out a way to get in on it.

This is especially obvious when you consider the low pay scale in which many in law enforcement find themselves. When you're only making $28 to $30 Gs a year, what's a little side venture? Let's say all you do is turn your head while a deal goes on—a cut for silence isn't that bad, is it? Many officers start down precisely this path. If you seize $500 from a suspect, who does it hurt if you only report $400? From there, getting deeper is just a matter of going with the flow. In his groundbreaking study, "The Economics of Prohibition," economist Mark Thornton explains in typical economist-speak that "When an official commits one act of corruption, the costs of additional acts decline, in a fashion similar to the marginal cost of production in a firm." In other words, pocketing that $100 gets easier and easier the more you do it.

Joel Miller, *WorldNetDaily*, October 25, 2000.

What role do institutional interests play in the drug war?

One year when I was police chief in San Jose, the city manager sent me a budget that contained no money for equipment. I politely told him that when you have a police department, you have to buy police cars, uniforms, and other equipment for the cops. He laughed, waved his hand, and said, "Last year you guys seized $4 million dollars. I expect you to do even better this year. In fact, you will be evaluated on that and you can use that money for equipment." So law enforcement becomes a revenue-raising agency and that takes, in too many cases, precedence over law enforcement.

From the perspective of the working police officer, how has the War on Drugs changed over the years?

It has become the priority of police agencies. It's bizarre. We make 700,000 arrests for marijuana a year. The public is not terrified of marijuana. People are terrified of molesters, school shootings, and people stalking women and children. The police are not putting the resources into those crimes where they could be effective if they gave them top priority.

Possession Versus Dealing

There's some controversy over whether the arrests for possession are really for possession or if they are for dealing but prosecuted as possession. Do you have any thoughts on that?

It's both true and false. Most low-level dealers are users, like the guy that we finally did bust after we let the addict go. He was an addict, too, and he was no better or worse than the guy we let go. But what we had actually done, which is standard operating procedure in the drug war, is let someone go who had committed a crime because they enticed someone else to commit a more serious crime.

The Role of Race in the War on Drugs

What role does race play in the War on Drugs?

The drug war is an assault on the African-American community. Any police chief that used the tactics used in the inner city against minorities in a white middle-class neighborhood would be fired within a couple of weeks.

It was a very radical change in public policy for the federal government to criminalize drugs in the early 20th century. Congress was reluctant to pass it because you had a very small federal government in 1914 and to interfere with the state police powers was a big deal. They couldn't get this legislation passed until they played the race card: They introduced letters and testimony that blacks were murdering white families; the police in the South were having trouble with "Negroes" because of these drugs; there were white women in "yellow" opium dens. The same prejudice popped up in 1937 when they outlawed marijuana.

If anyone tried to pass laws on those same bases today, they'd be condemned. Yet the laws that we have are the last vestiges of Jim Crow. You don't have to identify yourself as a bigot anymore—you can be for the drug war and you really are getting "them."

Do you think there's a greater risk in just questioning the operation of the War on Drugs than there is to testifying and going along with it in unethical ways?

For police chiefs, there is some wiggle room. They can support sterile needle exchanges, medical marijuana treatment, and education diversion instead of incarceration. But it's asking an awful lot for them to come out and say, "Look, this drug prohibition is a stupid thing we shouldn't have started in 1914 and it gets worse and worse every year." That's a big step for a police chief. That's asking them to commit career suicide.

Were you frustrated as a police chief with the constraints of the law?

Enormously. Police chiefs are sitting on kegs of dynamite. Many of them are really decent, progressive guys. They are worried about the disproportionate racial impact and the corruption. But there's nothing they can do. There's just too much money in it. You don't have the ability, regardless of the propaganda, to eliminate the code of silence. You don't have unlimited power. You have lots of constraints on how the police can discipline themselves, even for chiefs who are legitimately interested in doing so.

"The 'war on drugs' has replaced chattel slavery and de jure segregation as the main method of perpetuating America's long history of racial oppression."

The War on Drugs Promotes Racism

Deborah Small

The war on drugs is the newest tool to enslave African Americans and ensure their continued oppression, argues Deborah Small in the following viewpoint. Drug laws are enforced in a way that is racially biased, she contends. For example, while blacks make up just 13 percent of drug users, 74 percent of drug users sent to prison are black. In addition, sentences for using crack cocaine—typically used by blacks— are one hundred times harsher than those for using powdered cocaine—typically used by whites. Small is the director of public policy for the Lindesmith Center and former legislative director of the New York Civil Liberties Union.

As you read, consider the following questions:
1. According to Small, Latinos make up what percentage of the annual 700,000 arrests for marijuana?
2. In the author's opinion, why is it unlikely that there is a cause and effect relationship between drugs and crime?
3. What measures indicate that a shift has occurred in public attitudes about U.S. drug policy and the war on drugs, as cited by Small?

Deborah Small, "The War on Drugs Is a War on Racial Justice," *Social Research*, vol. 68, October 2001, p. 896. Copyright © 2001 by the New School for Social Research. Reproduced by permission of the publisher and the author.

More than 300 years ago, millions of African men, women, and children were forcibly removed from their homes and villages and exported to the European colonies as slaves. For many of their descendants living in the United States, the "war on drugs" has become the newest tool used to disrupt communities and generate today's slaves, a.k.a. prisoners. As political economist John Flateau graphically puts it: "Metaphorically, the criminal justice pipeline is like a slave ship, transporting human cargo along interstate triangular trade routes from Black and Brown communities; through the middle passage of police precincts, holding pens, detention centers and courtrooms; to downstate jails or upstate prisons; back to communities as unrehabilitated escapees; and back to prison or jail in a vicious recidivist cycle." It is surely relevant for understanding the current prison-industrial complex to know that slavery held a preeminent position in America's colonial economy. With over 2 million people behind bars, it is undisputed that today the principal engine driving the criminal justice system and the high rates of incarceration is the United States government's relentless and racist pursuit of the "war on drugs." The "war on drugs" has replaced chattel slavery and de jure segregation as the main method of perpetuating America's long history of racial oppression.

Biased Drug Laws

United States drug laws, while superficially neutral, are enforced in a manner that is massively and pervasively biased. In a country with "equal rights for all," one out of every three Black men in their twenties is now in prison or jail, on probation, or parole on any given day. Blacks constitute 13 percent of all drug users, but 35 percent of those arrested for drug possession, 55 percent of those convicted, and 74 percent of those sent to prison. In some states the racial disparity in arrests and convictions for drug offenses is much worse. In seven states, Blacks constitute between 75 and 90 percent of all drug offenders sent to prison. In New York, over 94 percent of inmates incarcerated for drug offenses are Black or Latino. In at least 15 states, Black men are sent to prison for drug offenses at rates that are from 20 to 57 times greater than for White men. The disproportionate arrests—and media coverage—feed the mistaken assumption that Blacks use drugs at higher rates than White and serve as justification for continued racial profiling. It is said that truth is the first casualty in war, and the "war on drugs" is no exception. Contrary to stereotype, "the typical cocaine user is white, male, a high school graduate employed full time and living in a small metropolitan area or suburb," to quote former drug czar William Bennett. By the government's count, more than 24 million Americans, mostly White, have used marijuana, cocaine, or some other illicit drug.

America's enforcement of its punitive drug policy has resulted in a system of apartheid justice. The population of Black and Brown men and women behind bars has caused our prisons to look like Antebellum plantations. Almost half the 700,000 annual marijuana arrests are of Latinos. This outcome is no coincidence; unequal treatment of minority group members pervades every stage of the criminal justice system. Black and Latino Americans are victimized by disproportionate targeting and unfair treatment by police and other front-line law enforcement officials; by racially skewed charging and plea-bargaining decisions by prosecutors; by discriminatory sentencing practices; and by the failure of judges, elected officials, and other criminal justice policymakers to redress the inequities that have come to permeate the system.

Federal financial support for education is no longer an option for many after a drug conviction. Two of the most populous states, New York and California, send more African-American and Latino men to prison each year than they graduate from colleges and universities. The government has sent a message that it prefers to incarcerate Black and Brown youth rather than to educate them. A drug conviction can also mean the loss of public assistance, access to public housing, civil service jobs, and other government services—sanctions that are seldom applied to other criminal offenses.

Communities of color are politically marginalized by laws that disenfranchise voters for felony convictions and provide economic incentives for rural communities to embrace prisons as a form of economic development. The prevailing theory about prisons in many locales is, "If we build them, they will come." Nationally, over 1.4 million Black men or 13 percent of the Black male adult population have been disenfranchised. During the last presidential election, an estimated 400,000 Black citizens of Florida were barred from voting because of a law enacted during Reconstruction permanently disenfranchising people with felony convictions.

Anderson. © by Kirk Anderson. Reprinted with permission.

Research has shown that drug and alcohol abuse rates are higher for pregnant White women than pregnant Black women, but Black women are about 10 times more likely to be reported to authorities under mandatory reporting laws. Between 1986 and 1991, the number of Black women incarcerated for drug offenses jumped 828 percent. Because of the "war on drugs," tens of thousands of children are permanently separated from the love and guidance of parents who have been incarcerated for drug offenses.

The racial bias of the drug war is exemplified by the 100-to-1 disparity in prison sentences for crack versus powder cocaine. As scientists and courts alike have declared, there is no rational basis for distinguishing between crack cocaine and powder cocaine. Nonetheless, in 1994, 90 percent of those convicted of federal crack cocaine offenses were Black, 6 percent Latino, and less than 4 percent White. Federal powder cocaine offenders were 30 percent Black, 43 percent Latino, and 26 percent White.

Crack sentencing is the modern equivalent of Jim Crow laws that reinforced postslavery discrimination. From the Civil War's end in 1865 until 1890, prison populations in most southern state penal systems were more than 95 percent Black people, many of whom were leased out to work in plantations, mines, factories, and railroads. One century later, prison populations are still disproportionately Black and Brown, prisoner labor is booming, and chain gangs have been resurrected in Alabama and Arizona. Multinational corporations own and operate private prisons, reaping profits on the backs of people of color.

Violent Crimes

Most Americans would agree that punitive drug policies relying on harsh sentences would have been changed long ago if Whites were incarcerated on drug charges at the same rate as Blacks and Latinos.

United States political leaders foster the racist myth that American violence is largely the product of illegal drugs and inner-city gangs. Yet, the United States has had the industrial world's highest homicide rates for some 150 years. The homicide rate for White American males, ages 15 to 24, was at least twice as high as the overall rate for males, ages 15 to 24, in 21 other countries for 1986–1987, including Canada, Japan, Israel, and the countries of Europe. In New York, state prosecutors have vigorously opposed any reforms of the draconian and punitive Rockefeller drug laws on the grounds that they are necessary to fight violent crime. However, research tells us that drug law offenders are overwhelmingly nonviolent: almost 80 percent of drug offenders sent to prison in New York in 1999 had never been convicted of a violent crime, significantly diminishing the likelihood of a cause and effect relationship between the reduction in violent crime and the enforcement of our drug laws. Vigorous prosecution of the drug laws coupled with mandatory sentencing has caused the state to imprison more people for nonviolent drug crimes each year than for violent crimes—hardly a strategy designed to maximize public safety.

The inherent racism in America's enforcement of its drug policy has reached crisis proportions. As a result there is a growing chorus of voices of African-American and Latino leaders who are challenging the political orthodoxy that public safety requires the incarceration of tens of thousands of Black and Brown people, mainly for nonviolent offenses. Parents and family members of incarcerated drug offenders are speaking out against laws that have stolen the lives of their loved ones at tremendous social and economic cost.

Changing Political Views

In Congress, many of the Black elected officials who supported mandatory minimum drug sentencing and many other instruments of the drug war have begun to question its impact on the communities they represent. In 1998, the Congressional Black Caucus (CBC) declared a "health emergency" in response to the crisis of HIV/AIDS in Black communities and lobbied the Clinton administration for increased funding to address it. The caucus also lobbied for federal funding for needle exchange as a public health intervention to reduce the spread of drug-related HIV—an important factor in the overall AIDS crisis. The CBC was ultimately successful in obtaining the former but not the latter. Yet, by raising the issue in Congress, it helped broaden the debate about United States drug policies. Key CBC members have introduced legislation to dismantle some of the excesses of the "war on drugs." Representative Maxine Waters (D.-CA) has introduced a bill to eliminate mandatory minimum sentencing for low-level drug offenders; Rep. Charles Rangel (D.-NY) has introduced a bill to eliminate the sentencing disparity for crack versus powder cocaine; and Rep. Al Wynn (D.-MD) has introduced legislation to expand the federal "safety valve" provisions that would allow a reduction in sentences for some incarcerated drug offenders.[1]

A growing number of public officials are willing to publicly challenge the prevailing orthodoxy regarding United

1. All of the bills were referred to a committee, where they died.

States drug policy. Most notably, Republican Governor Gary Johnson of New Mexico drew harsh criticism and ridicule when he first began speaking publicly about decriminalization and harm reduction. One year later, his administration introduced a comprehensive drug policy reform package that included increased funding for drug treatment, restoration of voting rights for former felons, and a program to reduce heroin overdose deaths. His approval rating in New Mexico is at an all-time high. Former California Congressman Tom Campbell, a moderate Republican, ran for the Senate on a platform that included a repudiation of the "war on drugs" and specifically the newly implemented Plan Colombia, the initiative that appropriates $1.3 billion to assist the Colombian government's fight against opponents in a civil war financed in part by drug trafficking. He lost in his bid to unseat Democrat Dianne Feinstein, but it was not because of his position on the drug war.

In recent years a definite shift has occurred in public attitudes about United States drug policy and an increased willingness to try alternative approaches to the "war on drugs." This shift is evident in the growing voter approval of ballot initiatives that allow the medical use of marijuana, limit the ability of law enforcement to seize assets of those "suspected" of involvement with drugs, and mandate that states opt for drug treatment over incarceration for minor drug offenders. These measures indicate recognition that drug addiction is primarily an illness best treated therapeutically rather than punitively.

Popular culture exhibits increasing criticism of the "war on drugs." Television shows such as *The West Wing* and movies such as *Traffic* have heightened public awareness of the drug war. *Traffic*, directed by Steven Soderburg, is an effective indictment of current policy, especially with respect to its impact on Mexico and America's other South American neighbors. Regrettably, it reinforces many of the racial stereotypes that served as the pretext for drug prohibition in the first place. Despite the film's flaws, we can hope that its success will catalyze a national conversation about the true casualties of our drug war and the expansion of the national movement to end it.

"Despite the hue and cry, there is nothing illegal about using race as one factor among others in assessing criminal suspiciousness."

The War on Drugs Does Not Promote Racism

Heather MacDonald

In the following viewpoint, Heather MacDonald argues that there is no credible evidence that racial profiling—when police officers stop and question a suspect because of his or her race—is used routinely in the war on drugs. However, she contends, race may be one of several factors that police officers consider when determining whether a suspect should be questioned further. Police often play the odds by pulling over someone who fits many of the components of a drug courier profile, such as the driver's race, the make of car, the direction traveled, and the number and ethnicity of passengers, she asserts. MacDonald maintains that there is nothing illegal about using race as one factor among many when assessing whether a crime has been committed. MacDonald is the John M. Olin Fellow at the Manhattan Institute and a contributing editor to *City Journal*.

As you read, consider the following questions:
1. What is the difference between "hard" and "soft" racial profiling, according to MacDonald?
2. What are some common identifying signs of drug couriers, according to the DEA as cited by the author?
3. What is the major flaw in studies that show minority drivers are stopped in disproportionate numbers, according to MacDonald?

Heather MacDonald, "The Myth of Racial Profiling," *City Journal*, vol. 11, Spring 2001. Copyright © 2001 by Heather MacDonald. Reproduced by permission.

The anti-"racial profiling" juggernaut must be stopped, before it obliterates the crime-fighting gains of the last decade, especially in inner cities. The anti-profiling crusade thrives on an ignorance of policing and a willful blindness to the demographics of crime. Yet politicians are swarming on board. In February, 2001, President George W. Bush joined the rush, declaring portentously: "Racial profiling is wrong, and we will end it in America."

Too bad no one asked President Bush: "What exactly do you mean by 'racial profiling,' and what evidence do you have that it exists?" For the anti-profiling crusaders have created a headlong movement without defining their central term and without providing a shred of credible evidence that "racial profiling" is a widespread police practice.

The ultimate question in the profiling controversy is whether the disproportionate involvement of blacks and Hispanics with law enforcement reflects police racism or the consequences of disproportionate minority crime. Anti-profiling activists hope to make police racism an all but irrebuttable presumption whenever enforcement statistics show high rates of minority stops and arrests. But not so fast.

"Hard" and "Soft" Profiling

Two meanings of "racial profiling" intermingle in the activists' rhetoric. What we may call "hard" profiling uses race as the *only* factor in assessing criminal suspiciousness: an officer sees a black person and, without more to go on, pulls him over for a pat-down on the chance that he may be carrying drugs or weapons. "Soft" racial profiling is using race as one factor among others in gauging criminal suspiciousness: the highway police, for example, have intelligence that Jamaican drug posses with a fondness for Nissan Pathfinders are transporting marijuana along the northeast corridor. A New Jersey trooper sees a black motorist speeding in a Pathfinder and pulls him over in the hope of finding drugs.

The racial profiling debate focuses primarily on highway stops. The police are pulling over a disproportionate number of minority drivers for traffic offenses, goes the argument, in order to look for drugs. Sure, the driver committed an infraction, but the reason the trooper chose to stop *him*, rather than the speeder next to him, was his race.

But the profiling critics also fault both the searches that sometimes follow a highway stop and the tactics of urban policing. Any evaluation of the evidence for, and the appropriateness of, the use of race in policing must keep these contexts distinct. Highway stops should almost always be color-blind, I'll argue, but in other policing environments (including highway searches), where an officer has many clues to go on, race may be among them. Ironically, effective urban policing shows that the more additional factors an officer has in his criminal profile, the more valid race becomes—and the less significant, almost to the point of irrelevance. . . .

Taking the Drug War to the Highways

The widespread pleas to stop drug violence led the Drug Enforcement Administration to enlist state highway police in their anti-drug efforts. The DEA and the Customs Service had been using intelligence about drug routes and the typical itineraries of couriers to interdict drugs at airports; now the interdiction war would expand to the nation's highways, the major artery of the cocaine trade.

The DEA taught state troopers some common identifying signs of drug couriers: nervousness; conflicting information about origin and destination cities among vehicle occupants; no luggage for a long trip; lots of cash; lack of a driver's license or insurance; the spare tire in the back seat; rental license plates or plates from key source states like Arizona and New Mexico; loose screws or scratches near a vehicle's hollow spaces, which can be converted to hiding places for drugs and guns. The agency also shared intelligence about the types of cars that couriers favored on certain routes, as well as about the ethnic makeup of drug-trafficking organizations. A typical DEA report from the early 1990s noted that "large-scale interstate trafficking networks controlled by Jamaicans, Haitians, and black street gangs dominate the manufacture and distribution of crack." The 1999 "Heroin Trends" report out of Newark declared that "predominant wholesale traffickers are Colombian, followed by Dominicans, Chinese, West African/Nigerian, Pakistani, Hispanic and Indian. Mid-levels are dominated by Dominicans, Colombians, Puerto

Ricans, African-Americans and Nigerians."

According to the racial profiling crowd, the war on drugs immediately became a war on minorities, on the highways and off. . . .

Black motorists today almost routinely claim that the only reason they are pulled over for highway stops is their race. Once they are pulled over, they say, they are subject to harassment, including traumatic searches. Some of these tales are undoubtedly true. Without question, there are obnoxious officers out there, and some officers may ignore their training and target minorities. But since the advent of video cameras in patrol cars, installed in the wake of the racial profiling controversy, most charges of police racism, testified to under oath, have been disproved as lies.

Studies Do Not Hold Up to Scrutiny

The allegation that police systematically single out minorities for unjustified law enforcement ultimately stands or falls on numbers. In suits against police departments across the country, the ACLU [American Civil Liberties Union] and the Justice Department have waved studies aplenty allegedly demonstrating selective enforcement. None of them holds up to scrutiny.

The typical study purports to show that minority motorists are subject to disproportionate traffic stops. Trouble is, no one yet has devised an adequate benchmark against which to measure if police are pulling over, searching, or arresting "too many" blacks and Hispanics. The question must always be: *too many compared with what?* Even anti-profiling activists generally concede that police pull drivers over for an actual traffic violation, not for no reason whatsoever, so a valid benchmark for stops would be the number of serious traffic violators, not just drivers. If it turns out that minorities tend to drive more recklessly, say, or have more equipment violations, you'd expect them to be subject to more stops. But to benchmark accurately, you'd also need to know the number of miles driven by different racial groups, so that you'd compare stops per man-mile, not just per person. Throw in age demographics as well: if a minority group has more young people—read: immature drivers—than whites do, expect more traffic stops of that group. The final analysis must then compare police deployment patterns with racial driving patterns: if more police are on the road when a higher proportion of blacks are driving—on weekend nights, say—stops of blacks will rise.

The Drug War Is Not Racially Biased

Some experts continue to misunderstand the racially unbalanced jail populations of those incarcerated for drug violations, making a blanket claim that the drug war somehow targets minorities instead of whites. While recognizing that unfortunately racism does exist in law enforcement as it does in much of the rest of today's society, those on the inside of narcotics enforcement know that this is not the predominant reason for the disparity in jail population. Rather, it is more directly connected to our philosophy of focusing the majority of our law enforcement efforts on arresting suppliers and dealers, the majority of whom happen to be minorities.

Michael Levine, in Timothy Lynch, ed., *After Prohibition: An Adult Approach to Drug Policies in the 21st Century*. Washington, DC: Cato, 2000.

No traffic-stop study to date comes near the requisite sophistication. Most simply compare the number of minority stops with some crude population measure, and all contain huge and fatal data gaps. An ACLU analysis of Philadelphia traffic stops, for example, merely used the percentage of blacks in the 1990 census as a benchmark for stops made seven years later. In about half the stops that the ACLU studied, the officer did not record the race of the motorist. The study ignored the rate of traffic violations by race, so its grand conclusion of selective enforcement is meaningless.

Flawed Studies

Only two studies, both by Temple University social psychologist John Lamberth, have attempted to create a violator benchmark. The ACLU used one to sue, successfully, the Maryland state police; a criminal defense attorney in New Jersey used the other to free 17 accused black drug traffickers. Lamberth alleged that blacks in Maryland and southern New Jersey were stopped at higher rates than their representation in the violator population would seemingly warrant. But he defined violator so broadly—in Maryland, traveling at least one mile, and in New Jersey, traveling at least six miles, over the speed limit—that he included virtually the entire driving population. Lamberth must not have spent much time talking to real cops, for his definition of violator ignores how police actually decide whom to stop. Someone gliding sedately at 56 mph in a 55 mph zone has a radically different chance of being pulled over than someone barreling along at 80. An adequate benchmark must capture the kind of driving likely to draw police attention. Despite his severely flawed methodology, Lamberth is in great demand as a racial profiling guru.

Taboo Question

Do minorities commit more of the kinds of traffic violations that police target? This is a taboo question among the racial profiling crowd; to ask it is to reveal one's racism. No one has studied it. But some evidence suggests that it may be the case. The National Highway Traffic Safety Administration found that blacks were 10 percent of drivers nationally, 13 percent of drivers in fatal accidents, and 16 percent of drivers in injury accidents. (Lower rates of seat-belt use may contribute to these numbers.) Random national surveys of drivers on weekend nights in 1973, 1986, and 1996 found that blacks were more likely to fail breathalyzer tests than whites. In Illinois, blacks have a higher motorist fatality rate than whites. Blacks in one New Jersey study were 23 percent of all drivers arrested at the scene of an accident for driving drunk, though only 13.5 percent of highway users. In San Diego, blacks have more accidents than their population figures would predict. Hispanics get in a disproportionate number of accidents nationally.

But though the numbers to date are incapable of telling us anything about racial profiling, that does not mean that it was not going on in some locations, at some times. Hard racial profiling in car stops—pulling over one speeder among many just because he happens to be black or Hispanic—has surely been rare. But conversations with officers in strong interdiction states such as New Jersey suggest that some troopers probably did practice soft racial profiling—

pulling someone over because driver *and* car *and* direction *and* number and type of occupants fit the components of a courier profile.

Playing the Odds

Over time, officers' experience had corroborated the DEA intelligence reports: minorities were carrying most of the drugs. An example of the patterns they noticed: a group of young blacks with North Carolina plates traveling south out of Manhattan's Lincoln Tunnel into New Jersey? Good chance they're carrying weapons and drugs, having just made a big buy in the city. Catch them northbound? Good chance they're carrying big money and guns. Some officers inevitably started playing the odds—how many, the numbers cannot yet tell us.

Despite the hue and cry, there is nothing illegal about using race as one factor among others in assessing criminal suspiciousness. Nevertheless, the initial decision to pull a car over should be based almost always on seriousness of traffic violation alone—unless, of course, evidence of other law-breaking, such as drug use, is visible. If the result is that drug couriers assiduously observe the speed limit, fine. But compared with most other policing environments, highways are relatively cueless places. In assessing the potential criminality of a driver speeding along with the pack on an eight-lane highway, an officer normally has much less to work with than on a city street or sidewalk. His locational cues—traveling on an interstate pointed toward a drug market, say—are crude, compared with those in a city, where an officer can ask if this particular block is a drug bazaar. His ability to observe the behavior of a suspect over time is limited by the speed of travel. In such an environment, blacks traveling 78 mph should not face a greater chance of getting pulled over than white speeders just because they are black and happen to be driving a car said to be favored by drug mules.

Soft racial profiling was probably not widespread enough to have influenced traffic-stop rates significantly. Nor will eliminating it quickly change the belief among many blacks that any time they get stopped for a traffic violation, it is because of their race. Nevertheless, state police commanders should eliminate any contribution that soft profiling may make to that perception, unless strong evidence emerges (as it has not so far) that soft profiling has had an extremely high success rate in drug interdiction. Far more is at stake here than the use of race in traffic stops. Specious anti-racial profiling analysis threatens to emasculate policing in areas where drug enforcement is on a far stronger basis.

A Bombshell Report

The most important victory of the anti-racial profiling agitators occurred not on the traffic-stop battlefield, but on the very different terrain of the searches that sometimes follow a stop. And here is where people who care about law enforcement should really start to worry. On April 20, 1999, New Jersey's then-attorney general Peter Verniero issued his "Interim Report of the State Police Review Team Regarding Allegations of Racial Profiling." It was a bombshell, whose repercussions haven't stopped yet.

"The problem of disparate treatment [of blacks] is real, not imagined," the report famously declared. Governor Christine Todd Whitman chimed in: "There is no question that racial profiling exists at some level." The media triumphantly broadcast the findings as conclusive proof of racial profiling not just in the Garden State but nationally. The *New York Times* started regularly referring to New Jersey's "racial bias" on the highways as incontrovertible fact. Defense attorneys and their clients celebrated as well. "Whenever I have a state police case, I file a suppression motion . . . alleging that the stop was based on color of skin and therefore illegal," a Trenton criminal defense attorney told the *New York Times*. "And now guess what? The state agrees with me!"

Shoddy Analysis

Yet the report's influential analysis is shoddy beyond belief. Contrary to popular perception, Verniero did not reach any conclusions about racial profiling in stops. His finding of "disparate treatment" is based on the percentage of "consent searches" performed on minorities *after* a stop has occurred. (In a consent search, the motorist agrees to allow the trooper to search his car and person, without a warrant or probable cause.) Between 1994 and 1998, claims the report, 53 percent of consent searches on the southern end of the New Jersey Turnpike involved a black person, 21 percent involved whites, and overall, 77 percent involved minorities. But these figures are meaningless, because Verniero does not include racial information about search requests that were denied, and his report mixes stops, searches, and arrests from different time periods.

But most important: Verniero finds culpable racial imbalance in the search figures without suggesting a proper benchmark. He simply assumes that 53 percent black consent searches is too high. Compared with what? If blacks in fact carry drugs at a higher rate than do whites, then this search rate merely reflects good law enforcement. If the police are now to be accused of racism every time that they go where the crime is, that's the end of public safety.

Periodical Bibliography

The following articles have been selected to supplement the diverse views presented in this chapter.

American Civil Liberties Union	"Race and the War on Drugs," 2003. www.aclu.org.
William J. Bennett	"Don't Surrender," *Wall Street Journal*, May 15, 2001.
Graham Boyd	"The Drug War Is the New Jim Crow," *NACLA Report on the Americas*, July/August 2001.
Clifton Coles	"Alternatives to Growing Drugs: First World Policies That Keep Food Cheap Counteract the War on Drugs," *Futurist*, May/June 2003.
Thomas G. Donlon	"Unintended Consequences: The War on Drugs Is a Self-Punishing Mistake," *Barron's*, June 24, 2002.
Steven Duke	"End the Drug War," *Social Research*, Fall 2001.
Economist	"Breaking Convention: Illicit Drugs," April 5, 2003.
Economist	"First, Inhale Deeply," September 2, 2000.
Christopher Lord	"The Poppies That Feed the Farmers," *New Statesman*, April 22, 2002.
Joseph D. McNamara	"The War America Lost," *Hoover Digest*, no. 1, 2000.
Kenneth B. Nunn	"Race, Crime, and the Pool of Surplus Criminality: Or Why the 'War on Drugs' Was a 'War on Blacks,'" *Journal of Gender, Race and Justice*, Fall 2002.
Peter Schrag	"Declaring War on the Drug War," *American Prospect*, September 24, 2000–October 2, 2000.
Peter Schrag	"A Quagmire for Our Time," *American Prospect*, August 13, 2001.
Joan Kennedy Taylor	"Ending the War on Drugs," *Free Inquiry*, Spring 2002.
Sanho Tree	"'They Do It Because They Make Money,'" *Sojourners*, May/June 2003.
Charles Van Deventer	"I'm Proof: The War on Drugs Is Working," *Newsweek*, July 2, 2001.
Kevin B. Zeese	"Just Say No to More Money for the Colombia Drug War," *Wall Street Journal*, April 28, 2000.

Is There a Link Between the War on Drugs and Terrorism?

Chapter Preface

Narco-terrorism is the trafficking in drugs to finance terror-ist activities. The classic example of a narco-terrorist is Pablo Escobar, leader of the Medellín cocaine cartel in Colombia, who was killed by a joint U.S.-Colombian secret military force in 1993. Escobar led an eight-year terrorist campaign during which he ordered the assassinations of judges, police officers, journalists, and presidential candidates. He also was responsible for the bombing of a commercial airplane. These terrorist activities were designed to pressure the Colombian government into banning extradition of drug traffickers to the United States.

More recent examples of narco-terrorists are members of the Taliban, the former ruling party of Afghanistan, and al-Qaeda, the Islamic terrorist group led by Osama bin Laden, which was responsible for the September 11, 2001, terrorist attacks. The Taliban permitted—and even taxed—the pro-duction of opium and heroin in Afghanistan and offered a safe haven to al-Qaeda, which cultivated poppies to produce opium and heroin. Profits from the sale of these drugs were used to finance the group's terrorist campaign.

After al-Qaeda's attacks on the World Trade Center and the Pentagon, the United States changed its focus in the war on drugs. It began a campaign publicly linking the war on drugs with the war on terrorism. According to the government's new antidrug campaign, people who buy illegal drugs are support-ing terrorism since many terrorist groups grow, manufacture, sell, and distribute drugs to finance their operations.

However, not everyone agrees that illegal drug users sup-port terrorism. Some observers contend that the war on drugs—sponsored by the U.S. government—is responsible for supporting terrorism. They argue that if drugs were le-gal, the high profits associated with illegal drugs would dis-appear, and trafficking in illegal substances would no longer support terrorists' activities.

The debate over whether illegal drug use or the war on drugs encourages terrorism is just one of the issues examined by the authors in the following chapter.

"Illegal drug production undermines America's culture; it funds terror; and it erodes democracy."

Illegal Drug Use Supports Terrorism

Asa Hutchinson

In the following viewpoint Asa Hutchinson argues that drug abuse supports terrorism and destabilizes governments. For example, the terrorists responsible for the September 11, 2001, terrorist attacks on America were supported by Afghanistan's ruling regime the Taliban, which generated revenue by taxing the production of heroin. In other countries, such as Colombia, revolutionaries traffic in illegal drugs to fund their wars against legitimate governments. The illegal drugs produced in foreign countries are destined for the United States, where, Hutchinson asserts, they threaten American culture and democracy. Hutchinson is the former director of the Drug Enforcement Administration.

As you read, consider the following questions:

1. According to Hutchinson, what two traits are needed to maintain democracy?
2. What are the three groups designated as terrorist organizations in Colombia, as cited by the author?
3. According to the State Department, how much does FARC receive each year from drug sales?

Asa Hutchinson, speech to the Heritage Foundation: Kathryn and Shelby Cullom Davis Institute for International Studies, Washington, DC, April 2, 2002.

W e understand from our study of history that the maintenance of democracy requires in essence two things: sacrifice and participation. We also know from our study of current culture that sacrifice and participation are contrary to the concept of drug use.

Drug abusers become slaves to their habits. They are no longer able to contribute to the community. They do not have healthy relationships with their families. They are no longer able to use their full potential to create ideas or to energetically contribute to society, which is the genius of democracy. They are weakened by the mind-numbing effects of drugs. The entire soul of our society is weakened and our democracy is diminished by drug use.

Many, in the name of freedom, say drug use should be permissible. The argument is that the government should have a hands-off attitude toward drug use and that if individuals exercise their freedom, they should be able to exercise it toward drug use or drug abuse. But that very freedom is jeopardized by drug addiction. When an addict takes cocaine, methamphetamine, heroin, or a whole host of other drugs, he is not only changing the chemistry of the body, but little by little diminishing the character of a nation.

But there's another dimension to the abuse of drugs. Not only does it weaken the United States, but it also supports attacks against the judicial system in Mexico. It funds terrorism in Colombia and generally destabilizes governments from Afghanistan to Thailand. . . .

The Facts on Drugs and Terrorism

Afghanistan. Let's briefly look at the facts of the connection between drugs and terrorism, starting with Afghanistan. Afghanistan, as you know, is a major source of heroin in the world, producing in the year 2000 some 70 percent of the world's supply of opium, which is converted to heroin.

The Taliban, the ruling authority [before 2002] benefited from that drug trade by taxing and, in some instances, being involved in the drug trafficking. Taxation was institutionalized to the extent that they actually issued tax receipts when they collected the revenue from the heroin traffickers.

I read from one receipt that was obtained during one of the

operations there:[1] "To the honorable road tax collectors: Gentlemen, the bearer of this letter who possesses four kilograms of white good has paid the custom duty at the ShinWa custom. It is hoped that the bearer will not be bothered further."

So it's clear that the Taliban benefited from the institutionalized taxation of heroin trafficking. Clearly, at the same time, the al-Qaeda network flourished from the safe haven provided by the Taliban.

Taken a step further, the DEA has also received multisource information that Osama bin Laden[2] himself has been involved in the financing and facilitation of heroin-trafficking activities. That is history now with the operation that has been taking place by our military in Afghanistan.

Now we can look to the future in Afghanistan. We're pleased that the interim president, Chairman Karzai, has banned poppy cultivation and drug production; but the United Nations, despite this ban that is currently in place, estimates that the area that is currently under cultivation could potentially produce up to 2,700 metric tons of opium in Afghanistan [in 2002]. This is an extraordinary concern to the DEA and the international community.

To put this in perspective, when you look at one area of the world producing 2,700 metric tons of opium, that contrasts to less than 100 metric tons of heroin being consumed in the United States. It's an overproduction in supply. It is a huge challenge that we face in Afghanistan, but it is also a tremendous opportunity for the international community to be energized, to be cooperative in their efforts to engage in that arena to impact the huge supply that comes out of Afghanistan.

South America

Colombia. In Colombia, we deal with three groups designated as terrorist organizations by the State Department: the revolutionary group called the FARC (Revolutionary Armed Forces of Colombia); the ELN (National Liberation Army);

---

1. After the September 11, 2001, terrorist attacks on America, the United States sent troops to Afghanistan to overthrow the ruling Taliban regime. The regime had been harboring al-Qaeda terrorists, who were responsible for the September 11 attacks. The United States was successful in overthrowing the Taliban.   2. Osama bin Laden is head of al-Qaeda.

and a paramilitary group, the AUC (United Self-Defenses of Colombia). At least two of those, without any doubt, are heavily engaged in drug trafficking, receiving enormous funds from drug trafficking: the AUC and the FARC.

Drug Money Funds Terrorists

There are a number of terrorist groups operating in Colombia—the three largest of which are the Revolutionary Armed Forces of Colombia (FARC), the United Self-Defense Groups of Colombia (AUC), and the National Liberation Army (ELN). Revenue that they receive from narcotics cultivation, taxation, and distribution provides at least half of the funding that the FARC and AUC rely on to support their terrorist activities. We estimate that the ELN derives much less of its funding from narcotics activities, and it may be no accident that the ELN is the smallest and least-powerful of the three groups. There would appear to be a direct correlation between drug activity and organizational viability and reach in Colombia. Certainly, the FARC's growth in numbers is directly related to the increase in its involvement with illicit drug cultivation and exploitation. . . .

Drug money finances attacks, such as the multiple-mortar attack on President [Alvaro] Uribe's inauguration which killed 21 residents of a poor Bogotá neighborhood. And without drug money, FARC units would not be able to arm themselves and dominate the amount of territory in southern Colombia that they do, a region where three American citizen contractors are still being held hostage by FARC units after their plane's engine malfunctioned, and they had to make an emergency landing.

Deborah McCarthy, hearing before the Senate Judiciary Committee, May 20, 2003.

In the case of the FARC, the State Department has called them the most dangerous international terrorist group based in the Western Hemisphere. [In 2002], the Department of Justice indicted three members of the 16th Front of the FARC, including their commander, Tomas Molina, on charges of conspiracy to transport cocaine and distribute it in the United States. It was the first time that members of a known terrorist organization have been indicted on drug trafficking charges.

The 16th Front operates out of a remote village in Eastern Colombia where they operate an air strip, where they engage in their trafficking activities, where they control all the operations in that particular arena. The cocaine that is transported by the 16th Front out of that area is paid for with currency, with weapons, and with equipment; and, of course, you know the activities that terrorist organization has been engaged in, in which they would use that currency, the weapons, and the equipment.

FARC and Cocaine

But the 16th Front is not the only front of the FARC that is engaged in drug trafficking activity. Ninety percent of the cocaine Americans consume comes from Colombia; the FARC controls the primary coca cultivation and processing regions in that country, and they have controlled it for the past two decades.

The State Department estimates that the FARC receives $300 million a year from drug sales to finance its terrorist activities.

In March of [2002], under the direction of President [Andres] Pastrana, the Colombian Army and the Colombian National Police reclaimed the demilitarized zone from the FARC, based upon intelligence the DEA was able to provide. The police went in, and in the demilitarized zone that was supposed to be a peaceful haven, they found two major cocaine laboratories. The police seized five tons of processed cocaine from that particular site, so you can imagine the enormity of this processing site. They destroyed the labs as well as a 200-foot communications tower that the FARC operated to use in their communications efforts.

Prior to the seizure, we knew the FARC was engaged in trafficking activities, but this is the first time we have had solid evidence that the FARC is involved in the cocaine trade from start to finish, from cultivation to processing and distribution.

We should understand that's it's not just Colombian citizens that are impacted by the terrorist activities. Since 1990, 73 American citizens have been taken hostage in Colombia, more than 50 by narco-terrorists; and since 1995, 12 American citizens have been murdered.

So we see a clear connection by al-Qaeda and the FARC using drug proceeds to finance their terrorist activities. They are not by any means the only two groups.

I mentioned the AUC, the paramilitary group in which Carlos Castagna, the leader of that organization, actually published a book in which he admitted that his paramilitary activities, his terrorist activities, were in fact funded to a large extent by drug trafficking. Let me assure you that he is under investigation.

An Extraordinary Impact on Lives

Peru. In Peru, you have the Shining Path. There's evidence that they were responsible for the car bombing that occurred [in 2002] that killed nine people prior to President [George W.] Bush's visit to Peru. They have historically also bene-fited from the taxation of coca cultivation in the region of Peru that they control.

So, yes, the facts demonstrate that drugs are a funding source for terrorism and violence against government. But it's not just the facts that are involved here; it's also the lives that are impacted to such an extraordinary extent.

Mexico. When I went to Mexico City in February [2002], I had a meeting with the Attorney General, Macedo de la Concha, and in that meeting, I shook hands with the prose-cutors that were on the back row as I was leaving. One of the prosecutors, Mario Roldan Quirino, was handling a case that we were involved in that was a multi-ton seizure of cocaine off of a fishing vessel. I shook hands with that prosecutor. Within one hour after I left Mexico City, Mario Roldon was shot 28 times outside of Mexico City and assassinated.

The Toll on Law Enforcement

In the first few months of 2002, 13 law enforcement officers have been murdered in Mexico. You say, "this may not be terrorism." When you're going after government officials, judicial officials, to impact the stability of a government, in my judgment, it is terrorism.

[In March 2002], I visited the Colombian National Po-lice—not just their police building, but also their hospital. In that hospital, I visited with five officers who were wounded in an attack by the FARC while they were doing coca eradication and providing protection for that operation.

Of those five that were wounded, four of these will return to duty. They are pleased to have that level of commitment. One will not return to duty. He was paralyzed for the rest of his life as the result of a car bomb attack near the United States embassy by a terrorist in Bogota. He was 24 years of age. All I could say to that young man was "Thank you."

America's understanding of the cost could best be demonstrated by "Just Say No to Drugs" in the United States.

America's National Interest

What is the national interest when it happens in faraway countries? It should be elementary: Drug production in Mexico, in Colombia, in Thailand, and in Afghanistan produces the supply of drugs that devastates our families and our communities.

The same illegal drug production funds that attack civilized society also destabilize democracies across the globe. Illegal drug production undermines America's culture; it funds terror; and it erodes democracy. And they all represent a clear and present danger to our national security.

"Prohibition alone is what makes the drug trade so profitable for terrorists."

The War on Drugs Supports Terrorism

Eugene Oscapella

Eugene Oscapella is a lawyer and founding member of the Canadian Foundation for Drug Policy. The following viewpoint is an excerpt of his testimony before the Senate of Canada Special Committee on Illegal Drugs. In it he asserts that many terrorist groups traffic in illegal drugs. Oscapella maintains that drug prohibition leads to huge mark-ups in the price of drugs, resulting in large profits for the terrorists who produce and traffic in the illegal substances. He argues that legalizing drugs would lower their price, thus reducing or eliminating the terrorists' profits, making it more difficult to fund terrorism.

As you read, consider the following questions:

1. Illegal drug production and trafficking make up what percentage of financing for Islamic fundamentalists, according to John Thompson?
2. According to the United Nations Office of Drug Control and Crime Prevention, what is the retail value of the illegal drug market per year?
3. How does the wholesale price of heroin in Afghanistan compare to the retail price in the United States, as cited by the author?

Eugene Oscapella, testimony before the Senate of Canada Special Committee on Illegal Drugs, Ottawa, Canada, October 29, 2001.

Some terrorism costs relatively little to accomplish. Carrying out the September 11 [2001] attacks in the United States may have cost only a few million dollars. However, many of the most feared forms of terrorism, the so-called weapons of mass destruction—biological, chemical and nuclear—can be very expensive to produce and deliver. For example, Aum Shinrikyo, a Japanese cult, put about 30 people and an estimated $30m into producing the chemical sarin that was released in the Tokyo subway in 1995. Profits from the production and sale of prohibited drugs can therefore be useful to terrorists planning these more expensive forms of terrorism. . . .

The Scope of the Problem

(All figures quoted are in US dollars, unless otherwise indicated.)

In May 2001, M. Alain Labrousse of the *Observatoire Geopolitique de Drogues (OGD)* in Paris appeared before this Committee to explain the links between drugs and terrorism. Terrorist organizations in almost 30 countries now finance their activities, to a greater or lesser extent, through the highly profitable trade in prohibited drugs. In particular, he explained how drug trafficking became increasingly important as a source of revenue for terrorist groups after the end of the Cold War. With the decline of state-sponsored terrorism, terrorist groups were forced to find other means to finance their activities. Where the agricultural climate permitted, this could mean drug production and sales. Even if the climate and terrain were not suitable for the production of drugs, terrorist groups could nonetheless reap enormous profits from the sale of prohibited drugs.

Said M. Labrousse, in a paper accompanying his presentation to the Senate Committee:

> Some [conflicts] . . . in Colombia, Afghanistan and Angola, were under way before the Cold War ended. The withdrawal of sister parties and powerful protectors not only made them less and less controllable, but also led some of the players to engage in mere predatory behaviour. In other cases, the collapse of Communist regimes caused new conflicts, in the former Yugoslavia, Azerbaidjan-Armenia, Georgia (Abkhazia, Ossetia), Chechnya and Tadjikistan. These conflicts, which

resulted in a weakening, and in some instances dislocation, of states also led to the development of drug trafficking.

In 1994, Interpol's chief drugs officer, Iqbal Hussain Rizvi, told Reuters News Agency that "Drugs have taken over as the chief means of financing terrorism."

In an interview shortly after the September 11, 2001, attacks in the United States, Mr. John Thompson of the Mackenzie Institute, a Canadian think tank studying terrorism and organized crime, suggested that the extent to which terrorist groups finance themselves through drugs varies widely. "With the Islamic fundamentalists, (it is) maybe 25 to 30 per cent. It's probably the single biggest money earner.". . .

The Value of the Global Trade in Illegal Drugs

The value of the global trade in illegal drugs is difficult to determine. However, the United Nations Office of Drug Control and Crime Prevention estimates that the retail value of the illegal market is $400 billion *per year*, which would put it ahead of the petroleum industry. *The Economist* magazine suggests that global retail sales are less, probably around $150 billion annually. (In comparison, Canada's annual real gross domestic product for 2001 is about $650 billion, and the US Department of Defense budget request for 2001 was about $290 billion.)

Both the lower and higher estimates of the value of the global drug trade point to an enormously rich source of financing for criminal and terrorist enterprises, amounting to hundreds of billions of dollars, possibly *more*, over the past few decades. . . .

Alliances Between Terrorist and Criminal Organizations

Increasingly, terrorist and criminal organizations (the line between them is blurred at best) are forming allegiances where their interests coincide. Together, criminal and terrorist organizations form an even more serious threat to peace and stability. Neil Pollard, Director of the US-based Terrorism Research Center, describes the extent of this threat:

> If terrorist interaction with transnational crime syndicates is successful enough—especially with narcotics traffickers—the

infrastructures of these interactions might be robust enough to provide terrorists with real opportunities for WMD [weapons of mass destruction] proliferation, including the introduction of a weapon of mass destruction into the United States. The implications of such an infrastructure are obvious.

How Prohibition Makes Drugs So Profitable

It costs very little to grow poppies, the raw material for opium and heroin, or to grow coca leaf, the raw material for cocaine. Yet users pay greatly inflated prices for the heroin and cocaine—often several thousand percent more than their cost of production. The inflated price of these drugs is purely a product of the black market produced by prohibiting them.

Without prohibition, these drugs would sell for much, much less. They would not present any significant opportunity for terrorist groups to profit from their production or sale.

The United Nations Office for Drug Control and Crime Prevention reports on the value of many drugs at different stages of production and sales. In Afghanistan, the world's largest producer of opium in the 1990s, the "farmgate" price of a kilogram of opium varied from $30–70. That is 3 to 7¢ a gram. Thanks to prohibition, a gram is sold in Canada for an average $39. That is from 550 to 1300 times the farmgate price.

Table 1: Opium

(all figures in $US)

Farmgate price per gram (Afghanistan)	3 to 7¢
Retail price per gram (in Canada)	$39.00
Multiple of retail to farmgate price	550 to 1300

United Nations Office for Drug Control and Crime Prevention, Global Illicit Drug Trends, 2001.

Heroin: In Afghanistan, the wholesale price of heroin produced from opium was an average of $2700 per kilo. In the United States, 40 percent pure heroin *wholesaled* for an average of $107,000 per kilo—about 40 times the wholesale price in Afghanistan. The same product *retailed* in the United States for an average $475,000 per kilo—175 times the wholesale price in Afghanistan.

Table 2: Heroin

(all figures in $US)

Wholesale price per kilo (Afghanistan: 1996)	$2,700
Wholesale price per kilo (Western Europe: 1996)	$60,000 (22 times Afghan wholesale price)
Wholesale price per kilo (US: 1999)	$107,000 (40 times Afghan wholesale price)
Retail price per kilogram (US: 1999)	$475,000 (175 times Afghan wholesale price)

United Nations Office for Drug Control and Crime Prevention, Global Illicit Drug Trends, 2001.

Cocaine: The leaf needed to produce a kilo costs about $400–600, according to Francisco Thoumi, author of an unpublished study of the Andean drugs industry. Says *The Economist* in a recent survey on illegal drugs, "by the time it leaves Colombia, the price has gone up to $1,500–1,800. On America's streets, after changing hands four or five times, the retail price for a kilo of cocaine works out at $110,000 [180 to 275 times the cost of the coca leaves], and in Europe substantially more."

The Economist notes that the "vast gap between the cost of producing the stuff and the price paid by the final consumer goes a long way to explaining why drugs policies so often fail."

Missing the Point

The media, police, policymakers and politicians often describe the problem simply as the financing of terrorism through the drug trade. Their analysis stops there. *They ignore the role of drug prohibition. Prohibition alone is what makes the drug trade so profitable for terrorists.*

Even some members of the Supreme Court of Canada seem to have been caught in the trap of attributing various harms (corruption, disease, violence) to the drug trade itself, rather than looking to the prohibition of drugs as a cause of these harms. This is particularly evident in the dissenting opinion of Cory and Major JJ. in the 1998 decision, *Pushpanathan v. Minister of Citizenship and Immigration:*

The established links between organized crime, terrorist organizations, arms dealing and drug trafficking compound the risks to security in individual countries and in the international community. According to the United Nations International Drug Control Programme, "[i]n situations of armed conflict, illicit drug revenues—or the drugs themselves—are regularly exchanged for arms." In some countries, such as Peru, trafficking organizations have formed alliances with guerrilla groups to ensure supplies of materials for processing. The financial and military power of these organizations threatens to undermine the political and economic stability of numerous countries, and indeed the entire international community.

The combined effects of the trade in illicit drugs have led one author to conclude that drug profits "do more to corrupt social systems, damage economies and weaken moral and ethical values than the combined effects of all other forms of crime. . . . The corrupting reach into government officials, politicians and the business community further endangers the stability of societies and governmental processes, and ultimately threaten political stability and even world order."

Further:

Drug trafficking has, throughout this century, been an international enterprise and hence an international problem. However, the ever increasing scale of the traffic, the apparent efficiency of organization and sophistication, the vast sums of money involved and the increasing links with transnational organized crime and terrorist organizations constitute a threat which is increasingly serious in both its nature and extent. Illicit drug trafficking now threatens peace and security at a national and international level. It affects the sovereignty of some states, the right of self-determination and democratic government, economic, social and political stability and the enjoyment of human rights.

These statements are accurate in part, but they are also very misleading because of their silence on an essential point—the role of prohibition in creating the harms identified in the statements. *Nowhere do the two dissenting judges appear to recognize that the* prohibition *of drugs is behind the profits, power, violence and corruption associated with the drug trade.*

Other Implications

The pursuit of prohibitionist foreign policies can generate serious consequential harms in the countries where those policies are imposed—defoliation and other environmental harms due to crop eradication, adverse health consequences from the use of herbicides on drug crops, loss of livelihood for already desperately poor farmers. Because prohibition is often enforced selectively, production and trafficking by some ideologically favored groups is tolerated, enhancing their power. This enables them to brutalize the population and destabilize the otherwise democratic governments. Colombia is perhaps the best example. Both the left-wing guerrillas and the right-wing paramilitaries in Colombia are known to profit extensively from the trade in cocaine.

Thus, prohibitionist policies both empower those domestic terrorist groups that are able to profit from the drug trade and often create other hardships within the countries on whom those policies are imposed. People undergoing such hardships can become hostile to the foreign powers that have encouraged these prohibitionist policies. This hostility can itself lead to violent acts, sometimes against Western interests and nationals abroad, and sometimes against them in their home countries. . . .

The events of September 11 have made it abundantly clear that we must do more than we have been doing to address the causes and mechanisms of terrorism. Relying on the same ideas, showing the same reluctance to look at the real impact of drug prohibition, will only continue to facilitate the terrorism that has rocked countries in other continents, and that may have just begun to rock our own.

Ending prohibition will not end terrorism. But it will remove the main, and often the easiest, source of funding for terrorism—the "cash cow" of the trade in prohibited drugs. This can be coupled with measures to attack other sources of funding for terrorists—greater vigilance about charitable donations and attempts to control extortion from members of expatriate communities.

American author Mike Gray states:

As Western civilization stands transfixed, paralyzed by the specter of twentieth-century Vandals devouring one country after another, it's important to remember that this particular impending catastrophe can be avoided with the stroke of the pen. The criminal enterprises that now encircle us . . . the powerful, ruthless combines that threaten to overwhelm the rule of law itself—all could be cut off by simply closing the black market money tap. . . . The prohibitionists have never been called to account for their part in this disaster. . . .

Gray's comments were directed primarily at how prohibition fosters the growth of criminal enterprises. Their logic applies equally to prohibition's role in financing terrorism.

We cannot maintain prohibition and yet still hope to deprive terrorist and criminal organizations of the profits associated with the drug trade. It is as simple as that.

The only measure with any realistic hope of stopping the flow of drug-related money to terrorists is to dismantle drug prohibition. After decades of propaganda about the evils of drugs, ending prohibition seems an extraordinary and almost unthinkable solution. It is not. If Canada is serious about attacking the financing of terrorism, it must get serious about abandoning prohibition.

The efforts of this committee should be directed at the admittedly challenging task of dismantling prohibition. It is completely irrational and destructive to maintain prohibition while acknowledging that prohibition fosters the trade that is now the leading source of funding for many terrorist and criminal organizations.

As long as we continue to pretend—and it is only pretending—that significantly reducing drug profits through traditional, failed, measures of supply and demand reduction is a realistic possibility, we will continue to provide terrorists an alarmingly simple source of enrichment. Without prohibition, the drug trade would not be a factor in terrorism. Because of prohibition, the drug trade is the major source of financing of terrorism. We must decide which version of drug policy we want—one that fosters terrorism and enriches terrorists, or one that does not.

"Drug-fighting must be part of the anti-terror strategy."

The War on Terror Must Be Fought in Conjunction with the War on Drugs

Robert Novak

Robert Novak argues in the following viewpoint that America's war on terror must be linked to the war on drugs. He claims that few countries are still willing or able to sponsor terrorist organizations, so the terrorists have had to look elsewhere for financing. According to Novak, many terrorist groups have discovered the benefits of producing and trafficking in illegal drugs: not only do the drugs produce large profits for the terrorists, but importing the drugs to western countries helps destroy those societies, a common aim of terrorist groups. Because of the link between terrorism and drugs, Novak maintains that the Drug Enforcement Administration should be included in counter-terrorism and homeland security activities. Novak is a syndicated columnist.

As you read, consider the following questions:
1. How many times did President George W. Bush discuss "narco-terrorism" in the three months immediately following the terrorist attacks on September 11, 2001, as cited by the author?
2. Which organization has appreciated the link between narcotics and terrorism, in Novak's opinion?
3. Why is it increasingly more difficult for terrorist organizations to receive financing from state sponsors?

America's war on terrorism ought to be linked inextricably to the war on drugs. It is not. That unfortunate failure, making it more difficult to defeat either scourge, is reflected in two anomalies.

• George W. Bush, omnipresent and eloquent in exhorting his fellow citizens to combat terror, since [the September 11, 2001, terrorist attacks] has mentioned narcotics hardly at all. Not once in his daily rhetoric . . . has the president used the phrase "narco-terrorism."

• The Drug Enforcement Administration (DEA), widely considered to have the best U.S. intelligence operations, has no seat at the inter-agency table in fighting terrorism. It never did, and the attacks of Sept 11 did not change anything.

These facts of life are the background to an unprecedented narco-terrorism symposium convened by the DEA's aggressive new administrator, former Rep. Asa Hutchinson, and held at the DEA headquarters in Arlington, Va. Criticism was restrained and indirect, but the consensus was clear that drug-fighting must be part of the anti-terror strategy.

The Link Between Terrorism and Drugs

The DEA has always appreciated the nexus between terror and narcotics, but not the State Department or CIA. Accordingly, the U.S. government for years turned a blind eye to the fact that Colombia's FARC [Revolutionary Armed Forces of Colombia] guerrillas from the start have been financed by illegal narcotics. The Taliban, which supported Osama bin Laden and al Qaeda [the terrorists responsible for September 11], has been financed by the opium trade to Europe. While U.S. policymakers still talk at length about state-sponsored terrorism, support now is more likely to come from the poppy seed than a government sanctuary.

Raphael Perl, narco-terrorism expert for the Congressional Research Service, told [the] symposium that "income from the drug trade has become increasingly important to terrorist organizations." He added: "State-sponsors are increasingly difficult to find. What world leader in his right mind will risk global sanctions by openly sponsoring al Qaeda or funding it?" Steven Casteel, DEA chief of intelligence, agreed: "State-sponsored terrorism is diminishing.

These organizations are looking for funding, and drugs bring one thing: quick return on their investment."

Narcotics provide more than a way to finance terrorism, in the DEA's view. Al Qaeda expands ABC—atomic, biological and chemical—to ABCD, with drugs added, according to Casteel. "Drugs are a weapon of mass destruction that can be used against Western societies and help bring them down," he said.

Missed Opportunities

On Sept. 7 [2001], DEA agents seized 53 kilos of Afghan heroin distributed by Colombians. "I would argue," said Casteel, "that we've been under attack in this country for a long time, and it didn't start on Sept. 11." Considering DEA's experience, it would seem natural that its representatives would immediately be put on the high command of the new war against terrorism. They were not, and still have not.

A Threat to National Security

Drug trafficking [is] a threat to the security of the United States. For one, it is no secret that narco-traffickers have working relationships with insurgent and terrorist organizations. The "narco-terrorism" relationship provides insurgent/terrorist organizations with the funding to expand their operations, as well as providing greater security, firepower, transportation, and organizations to the traffickers. However, drug trafficking is a silent, almost disregarded form of obtaining revenues for terrorism. Anti-American organizations can quickly finance a substantial force with drug money. . . .

The fact that drug traffickers and terrorists can and do work side by side also indicates that the Homeland Security intelligence apparatuses of terrorism and counter-drug issues could become one and the same.

Douglas J. Davids, *ROA National Security Report*, August 2001.

Larry Johnson, a former CIA official who was a high-ranking State Department counter-terrorism expert during the first Bush administration, told the symposium: "I can say, hands down, that the best intelligence we have on the ground overseas is DEA and yet, after all of the time that I've been involved with counter-terrorism, not once have I seen a DEA body sitting at the table, at the CSG (Counter-terrorism and Security Group) meetings which go on at the White House, where you're talking about combating terrorism." Nor are they there today.

No wonder the president never uses the words narco-terrorism. What is lost by this silence is the leverage of the presidential bully pulpit to fight drugs. The DEA symposium was called "Target America: Traffickers, Terrorists and Your Kids." The "kids" part was discussed by Stephen Pasierb of the Partnership for a Drug-Free America. He presented polling data showing a rare conjunction between generations: a mutual inclination by parents and children to believe that illegal drugs finance terrorism.

That opportunity can be exploited by the government's massive megaphone, especially the presidential bully pulpit. "The understanding of this link (between narcotics and terrorism) is essential," said Pasierb, "and that's what our leaders can do. Leadership in this nation can help our people understand." The wonder is that the blase attitude toward narcotics in high places that marked the Clinton administration has not totally disappeared under President Bush.

*"The picture [of the war on drugs] is of a
policy that has failed to protect us, and
diverted the attention of our guardians
away from our real enemies."*

The War on Drugs Distracts
from the War on Terror

Eric E. Sterling

Eric E. Sterling is president of the Criminal Justice Policy
Foundation in Washington, D.C. In the following viewpoint
Sterling maintains that law enforcement agencies are spending too much time and money on drug intervention instead
of fighting crime and terrorism. Their efforts in the war on
drugs are wasted, he asserts; deaths from drug abuse have
doubled, drug purity has increased, and illegal drugs are easier to obtain now than they were thirty years ago. Therefore,
he contends, drugs should be legalized and regulated so that
law enforcement can focus on fighting terrorism.

As you read, consider the following questions:

1. What percentage of the FBI's effort was devoted to
   fighting drugs in 1998–2000, as cited by the author?
2. How many arrests are made each year for drug offenses,
   according to Sterling?
3. How much did drug users spend on illegal drugs in
   2000, as cited by the author?

F BI Director Robert S. Mueller notes that the absence of a specific warning about September 11, 2001 [the terrorist attacks], "doesn't mean that . . . there weren't dots that should have been connected . . ." The cliche of the season is "connecting the dots." Of course in the real world the dots aren't numbered as they are in a children's puzzle, so you have to look harder.

The Dots

Dot: In 1998, 1999 and 2000, 30% of the FBI's entire effort was devoted to fighting drugs. More than 20% of the FBI was fighting drugs in 2001.

Dots: Enormous efforts of key border protection agencies are diverted to finding drugs: Customs Service, 35–45%; Immigration, 15%; Coast Guard, 12–18%; Secret Service 11–13%; Federal Law Enforcement Training Center, 60%.

Dot: The Defense Department spends almost $1 billion a year fighting the drug trade.

Dot: CIA-run air interdiction program shoots down civilian aircraft in Peru [in April 2001] killing a missionary and her daughter.

Dot: 1.5 million arrests for drug offenses each year, a majority of them for marijuana possession.

Dot: The drug abuse death rate has more than doubled since 1979, and the number of deaths per year has almost tripled.

Dot: Nearly three million hard core drug addicts remain untreated year after year.

Dot: The average purity of heroin sold in the street has increased 500% since 1981.

Dot: Hospital emergency room admissions for drugs are up 50% in the past decade.

Dot: High school kids reported that drugs like marijuana and heroin were easier to get in 1998 than at any time since 1975.

Dot: U.S. drug users spent $64 billion on illegal drugs in 2000.

Dot: Drug prohibition proceeds help finance terrorists like the FARC and AUC, the guerrillas and paramilitaries in Colombia. Regulated and licensed businesses, including coffee, alcohol, tobacco, flowers, etc., do not finance terrorists.

Dot: FBI, CIA and law enforcement missed the red flags that were up before September 11.

A Failed Policy

The picture that emerges is an enormous effort to fight drugs with very expensive law enforcement and intelligence resources. On the key objectives of saving lives, reducing injuries, and keeping drugs out of the hands of kids, the problem gets worse and worse.

The picture is of a policy that has failed to protect us, and diverted the attention of our guardians away from our real enemies.

Wasted Resources

One has to smoke something pretty strong to conclude that someone who uses marijuana to fight life-threatening AIDS wasting syndrome somehow is in cahoots with al Qaeda. . . .

As the U.S. confronts budget deficits and a growing surplus of enemies dedicated to America's destruction, Washington must rearrange its priorities. Neither cancer patients nor classic rockers who use marijuana will murder another 3,000 innocent civilians in cold blood. Every federal agent who stops pot smokers from lighting up is one less agent who can prevent Americans from blowing up.

Deroy Murdock, *National Review Online*, February 19, 2002.

Interpretation of the picture: It's time to end the war on drugs. It's time to change the law to regulate and control drugs, not empower and enrich criminals and terrorists taking advantage of prohibition. We should license drug users, sellers and manufacturers to reduce deaths, injuries and crime. We should also end failed prevention programs that are pedagogically flawed but politically perfect, and provide drug treatment to the 3 million untreated hard core addicts.

The President's budget for the next fiscal year proposes 9.7% of the FBI effort to be devoted to fighting drugs. It's time for that number to be zero.

Periodical Bibliography

The following articles have been selected to supplement the diverse views presented in this chapter.

Marc Chernick	"Just Say No: The War on Terror Will Fail Unless the United States Heeds the Lessons from Its Disastrous War on Drugs," *WorldLink*, July/August 2002.
Gary Fields	"Move to Link Drug, Terror Wars Draws Flak," *Wall Street Journal*, April 1, 2002.
David R. Henderson	"Supporting the Drug War Supports Terrorists," *Reason*, July 2002.
Richard Jerome and Ron Arias	"The Shadows Knows," *People Weekly*, October 21, 2002.
Dennis Jett	"Remember the Drug War? A Casualty of Terrorism You Haven't Heard Much About," *Washington Post*, January 13, 2002.
Stephen Johnson and Jason Hagen	"Should the United States Continue Aiding Colombia's Counterinsurgency Efforts?" *CQ Researcher*, March 14, 2003.
Allison North Jones	"Strong Views, Pro and Con, on Ads Linking Drug Use to Terrorism," *New York Times*, April 2, 2002.
Wendy Kaminer	"Drugs, Terror, and Evictions," *American Prospect*, June 3, 2002.
James Kitfield	"Giving War a Chance," *National Journal*, June 1, 2002.
Michael Massing	"Home-Court Advantage: What the War on Drugs Teaches Us About the War on Terrorism," *American Prospect*, December 3, 2001.
Kenneth E. Sharpe and William Spencer	"Refueling a Doomed War on Drugs: Flawed Policy Feeds Growing Conflict," *NACLA Report on the Americas*, November/December 2001.
Jacob Sullum	"Drugs and Thugs: The U.S. Subsidy for Terrorists," *Reason*, December 2001.
Mark Thomas	"In Colombia, the U.S. Turns a Blind Eye to Drugs Barons and Arms Them," *New Statesman*, October 22, 2001.
Norah Vincent	"Change Tactics or Concede to Terrorism," *Los Angeles Times*, October 3, 2001.
Washington Post	"Drug Users as Traitors," February 12, 2002.

CHAPTER 3

Which Policies Are Working in the War on Drugs?

Chapter Preface

The Drug Abuse Resistance Education (DARE) program was created by the Los Angeles Police Department in 1983 to teach children how to resist peer pressure to use illegal drugs. Twenty years later, DARE is the country's most popular drug-education program; approximately 80 percent of the school districts in the United States include DARE in their curriculum.

DARE leaders and supporters believe that the program has many benefits. They assert that children who participate in DARE have an enhanced awareness of the dangers of illegal drugs. DARE also improves relations between students, parents, and police officers, they say. Advocates of DARE assert that the program shows children that they have a choice in how to live their lives. The police officers who lead the DARE program also teach children how to handle peer pressure and work to improve their self-esteem. Furthermore, DARE leaders maintain that when the program is combined with other drug-prevention initiatives, youth drug use falls dramatically.

Not everyone is convinced of DARE's success in reducing drug use, however. Some people contend that there is no evidence that drug education programs have reduced drug problems. They cite studies finding that students who were enrolled in DARE are just as likely to use drugs as students who were not involved in DARE. They claim that any deterrent effect disappears by the time students are in high school. Furthermore, new studies have found that parental attitudes are the most important factor influencing whether or not children take drugs.

Drug education programs are just one strategy used to combat drug use in the war on drugs. Other policies examined by the authors in the following chapter include mandatory minimum sentences for drug offenders and drug courts that offer treatment instead of incarceration for drug users.

*"Mandatory minimum sentences put steel
in the spine of our criminal justice system."*

Mandatory Minimum Sentences Are an Effective Strategy in the War on Drugs

David Risley

David Risley is the assistant U.S. attorney for the central district of Illinois. In the following viewpoint Risley asserts that when major drug crimes become routine in a judge's jurisdiction, his or her tendency is to become desensitized to the seriousness of drug crimes, and to begin handing out lighter sentences. These lenient sentences are unfair to those who receive stiffer sentences for the same crime in a different jurisdiction or from a different judge. Mandatory minimum sentences are designed to prevent such disparities in sentencing. Risley also contends that complaints about "harsh" sentences for drug crimes are unfounded.

As you read, consider the following questions:
1. Why does Risley believe that drug dealers should be imprisoned instead of treated?
2. What are the two levels of mandatory minimum sentences, according to the author?
3. What is the profit for a dealer who sells 900 pounds of marijuana, as cited by Risley?

The purpose of mandatory minimum sentences is to prevent the judicial trivialization of serious drug crimes. They do that well, to which some protest. Because the federal sentencing system is the model most often cited, it will be used for illustration throughout the following discussion.

A Wide Disparity in Sentencing

Before the advent of mandatory minimum sentences in serious drug cases, federal judges had unbridled discretion to impose whatever sentences they deemed appropriate, in their personal view, up to the statutory maximum. Because individual judges differ widely in their personal views about crime and sentencing, the sentences they imposed for similar offenses by similar defendants varied widely. What some judges treated as serious offenses, and punished accordingly, others minimized with much more lenient sentences.

Ironically, more lenient sentences became particularly prevalent in areas with high volumes of major drug crime, such as large metropolitan and drug importation centers. Perhaps the sheer volume of cases in such areas led to a certain degree of desensitization. When serious crime becomes routine, there is human tendency to treat it routinely, and sentences often drop accordingly. In some areas across the country, that phenomenon can even be seen with crimes such as murder.

While the ideal is that sentences be perfectly personalized by wise, prudent, and consistent judges to fit every individual defendant and crime, the reality is that judges are human, and their wide human differences and perspectives lead to widely different sentences, if given completely unbridled discretion.

Such wide disparity in sentencing is inherently unfair, at least to those who receive stiff sentences for crimes for which others are punished only lightly. But such inconsistency was welcomed by drug dealers, since it meant they could hope for a light sentence for serious drug crimes. That, of course, created a much bigger problem.

Leniency Leads to More Crime

Drug dealers are risk takers by nature. Lack of certainty of serious sentences for serious crimes encourages, rather than deters, such risk takers to elevate their level of criminal activity in the hope that, if caught, they will be lucky enough to draw a lenient judge and receive a lenient sentence. The only possible deterrence for people who are willing to take extreme risks is to take away their cause for such hope.

Mandatory Minimums Help Law Enforcement

In narcotics enforcement, mandatory minimum sentences are reserved principally for serious drug offenders, based on the quantity of narcotics distributed, and for related firearms violators. Criminals with prior drug felony convictions or who have operated a continuing criminal enterprise also receive stricter sentences.

These crimes threaten our national safety and must be prosecuted vigorously. Mandatory minimums assist in the effective prosecution of drug offenses by advancing several important law enforcement interests. . . .

Mandatory minimums increase the certainty and predictability of incarceration for certain crimes, assuring uniform sentencing for similarly situated offenders. The Department [of Justice] believes that uniform and predictable sentences deter certain types of criminal behavior by forewarning the potential offender that, if apprehended and convicted, his punishment will be certain and substantial. Mandatory minimum sentences also incapacitate serious dangerous offenders for substantial periods of time, thereby enhancing public safety.

John Roth, testimony before the Subcommittee on Criminal Justice, Drug Policy, and Human Resources, May 11, 2000.

Some counter that drug dealers are undeterrable by criminal sanctions because they sell drugs to support their own addictions, and so should be treated for their addictions rather than imprisoned. While there may be some merit to that argument for many low-level street dealers, it is generally untrue of their suppliers, and even many other street dealers. Most dealers and distributors at any substantial level do not use drugs themselves, or do so only infrequently. They are exploiters and predators, and users are their captive prey. Drug dealing is a business. As in any other business, drug addicts are unreliable and untrustworthy, especially around drugs, and so make poor business partners. Because drug dealers usually run their operations as high-risk businesses, they necessarily weigh those risks carefully, and so are deterrable when the risks become too high. Many dealers who used to carry firearms, for example, now avoid doing so when they are selling drugs due to the high mandatory federal penalties when guns and drugs are mixed.

However, drug dealers seldom view the risks as too high when they see reason to hope for a light sentence. Congress, however, can, and did, step in to take away that hope. By establishing mandatory minimum sentences for serious drug offenses, Congress sent a clear message to drug dealers: no matter who the judge is, serious crime will get you serious time.

To those who do not view crimes subject to mandatory minimum sentences as serious, including drug dealers and their support systems, that message is objectionable. To most, it is welcome. Mandatory minimum sentences put steel in the spine of our criminal justice system.

Two Levels of Mandatory Minimum Sentences

The natural question which follows is, what level of dealing must defendants reach before being subject to mandatory minimum sentences, and what are those sentences? The answer varies with the type of drug and whether the defendant is a repeat offender.

In the federal system, there are two levels of mandatory minimums, with each level doubling for defendants with prior convictions. The first tier requires a minimum sentence of imprisonment for five years (10 with a prior felony drug conviction), and the second tier requires a minimum of 10 years (20 with one prior felony drug conviction, and mandatory life with two such prior convictions). Of that, defendants can receive a reduction in the time they serve in prison of only 54 days per year as a reward for "good behavior," which means they must actually serve about 85% of their sentences.

For a prior drug offense to be considered a felony, it must be punishable by more than one year. In the federal system and most states, a drug offense is rarely classified as a felony unless it involves distribution of the drugs involved, or an intent to do so. For most practical purposes, therefore, a prior felony conviction for a drug such as marijuana can be read to mean a prior conviction for distribution. And, since most small distribution cases are reduced to misdemeanor simple possession (personal use) charges as part of plea bargains, especially for first-time offenders, a prior felony drug conviction for a drug such as marijuana usually means the prior conviction either involved a substantial amount of the drug or a repeat offender undeserving of another such break.

Not Low-Level Offenders

In the case of marijuana, those who oppose mandatory minimum sentencing on so-called "humanitarian" grounds seldom mention that, to be eligible for even a five-year minimum sentence, a defendant must be convicted of an offense involving at least 100 kilograms (220 pounds) of marijuana, or, in the case of a marijuana growing operation, at least 100 plants. Such defendants are not low-level offenders.

With marijuana available at the Mexican border in Texas for wholesale prices between $600 to $1100 per pound, and selling in most areas at a retail price of between $1200 to $2000 per pound, and with any reasonably healthy cultivated marijuana plant producing at least one and sometimes two pounds of finished product, eligibility for even the lowest mandatory minimum sentence requires conviction of an offense involving between $132,000 to $440,000 worth of marijuana, or plants capable of producing marijuana worth a bulk retail price of between $120,000 to $450,000.

To be eligible for the next, 10-year tier of minimum sentence, a defendant must be convicted of an offense involving 1000 kilograms (1.1 tons) of marijuana or 1000 marijuana plants. Even at a low wholesale price of $600 per pound, such offenses involve marijuana worth at least $1.3 million. One kilogram equals 2.2 pounds. Conversely, one pound equals 453.6 grams, and one ounce equals 28.35 grams.

It would be difficult to describe any offense involving between $120,000 to $450,000 worth of drugs as undeserving of even a five year prison sentence. Yet, those who oppose mandatory minimum sentences for marijuana and other drug offenses do just that, usually by attempting to convey the false impression the criminals they are attempting to protect are only low-level offenders.

High Profits

In examining the deterrent potential of such mandatory minimum sentences, one must consider that the profit potential for marijuana offenses is relatively high, and the penalties relatively low, which makes marijuana an attractive drug in which to deal, as evidenced by its widespread availability. To illustrate, if a dealer bought 200 pounds of marijuana in Texas for $900 per pound for a total of $180,000, transported it to the Midwest and sold it for as low as $1400 per pound, for a total of $280,000 with minimal overhead, the profit for just one such trip would be $100,000. When the street-level price of between $125 to $300 per ounce is considered, or the lower acquisition costs if the marijuana is grown by the dealer himself, the profit potential for such a venture can be huge, and yet still not involve enough drugs to trigger even the lowest mandatory minimum penalty. Since the chance of getting caught for any single trip of that sort is relatively low, the prospect of a quick $100,000 profit lures plenty of eager dealers, even with the risk of spending close to five years in prison.

Of course, if drug dealers are undeterrable, as the actions of many demonstrate they are, the only realistic options left are to either give up and allow them to ply their predatory trade unhindered (the legalization "solution"), or incapacitate them with even longer sentences.

The debate, it would seem, should be about whether the mandatory minimum penalties for marijuana offenses are currently too lenient, not too harsh.

> *"We are not catching drug kingpins. We are catching the little guys, the girlfriends, the mules, and we are sending them to prison for 5 years, 10 years, and often much longer."*

Mandatory Minimum Sentences Are Unfair

Julie Stewart

Julie Stewart is president of Families Against Mandatory Minimums. In the following viewpoint she argues that mandatory minimum sentences are unfair to convicted defendants and the judges who must sentence them. Under mandatory minimum sentencing guidelines, judges can no longer use their discretion to determine an appropriate sentence for a drug offender. Instead, Congress has determined what each defendant's sentence should be, regardless of any mitigating circumstances. Sending these drug offenders to prison for five or ten years for minor crimes destroys their lives and the lives of their families. Mandatory minimum sentences must be repealed, she concludes.

As you read, consider the following questions:

1. How many marijuana plants were the author's brother and his friends growing when they were arrested?
2. Why did Jeff's friends receive probation when Jeff was sentenced to five years in prison, according to Stewart?
3. What percentage of the federal prison population consulted of drug offenders in 1986?

Julie Stewart, "Effects of the Drug War," *After Probation: An Adult Approach to Drug Policies in the 21st Century*, edited by Timothy Lynch. Washington, DC: Cato Institute, 2000. Copyright © 2000 by the Cato Institute. All rights reserved. Reproduced by permission.

Ten years ago I worked as director of public affairs for the Cato Institute. I had no idea then that I would one day become an expert on sentencing, but life has a way of throwing you curve balls. The curve ball I received was the sentencing and incarceration of my only brother, Jeff, in 1990 for growing marijuana.

His case is not the worst I have seen, nor is it the best. But at the time, it was the only one I knew about. Even today it still illustrates what is wrong with the mandatory minimum sentencing laws that I have spent the past nine years trying to overturn.

Jeff's Case

Jeff was leading a relatively unproductive life in Washington state. He was 35 years old and he was smoking marijuana every day when he and two friends decided they could grow their own pot, have a ready supply, and sell some of it to their friends. They set up a grow-room in a garage on property that Jeff owned and on which his two friends lived. They filled the room with as many little pots as would fit (about 365) and started their seedlings.

When the plants were about 5–6 inches tall, the friends who lived on the property invited the neighbor over to smoke a joint and then showed him the grow-room. The neighbor subsequently called the police and received a $1,000 reward for turning in the pot-growers. When the two men were arrested, they quickly gave up my brother's name in exchange for a reduction in sentence. The system worked beautifully.

Both of the men had prior felony convictions for drug offenses, and one of them had served time in a California prison for a drug offense. But in exchange for informing on my brother, they both got probation. If they had not provided "substantial assistance" to the prosecutor, they would have received the same sentence that Jeff did (or perhaps more, due to their priors). Instead, Jeff ended up holding the bag and received a federal prison sentence of five years, without parole. When Jeff was arrested, I was at Cato working. I vividly remember his phone call from jail to my office. When he told me that he had been arrested for growing marijuana, my first thought was "how stupid of you"; my second thought was "well, it's *only* marijuana." Little did I know that there is no such thing as "only" marijuana anymore.

The Sentence

Jeff ended up pleading guilty because the prosecutor threatened him with a 15-year sentence if he took his case to trial. This is a common tactic—they charge you with every possible offense, then offer to drop some of them if you agree to plead guilty. The statistics show that the government wins in 96 percent of the cases that go to trial. Even for the innocent, the risk is very high. Jeff was not innocent and knew he would lose at trial, so he pleaded guilty. In exchange, he was given a "mere" five years in prison, instead of the possible 15 years.

At Jeff's sentencing, his judge, Judge Robert McNichols from the Eastern District of Washington (who is now deceased) made a strong statement opposing the sentence he was forced by law to impose on Jeff. He described being a senior district court judge who had been on the bench for 25 years, yet deemed unfit by act of Congress to determine the appropriate sentence in my brother's case. Instead, a young federal prosecutor straight out of law school was empowered to tell him what sentence he must deliver.

Those were the comments that motivated me to leave the Cato Institute and start a nonprofit organization to change mandatory minimum sentencing laws [Families Against Mandatory Minimums (FAMM)]. What kind of a justice system was it where the judge no longer had sentencing power? And why was Jeff prosecuted federally in the first place—he had not crossed state lines; it was not a DEA [Drug Enforcement Administration] bust. All of this was completely contrary to everything I had learned about our criminal justice system in school. I was outraged that American voters had allowed this to happen and that nothing was being done to stop it.

Mandatory Minimums Are Not New

I've learned a lot in the past nine years. The first thing I learned is that mandatory minimum sentencing laws are not new—they've been around for over 200 years. In 1991, the U.S. Sentencing Commission published a report on mandatory minimum sentences at the request of Congress. The report lists all of the mandatory minimum sentencing laws on the books, starting in 1790 when piracy on the high seas resulted in a prison sentence of life without parole.

Herblock. © 2000 by Herbert Block. Reprinted with permission.

There are more than 100 separate federal mandatory minimum penalty provisions located in 60 different criminal statutes. They make for a fascinating historical tour of the crime du jour:

- In 1857, refusal to testify before Congress resulted in a sentence of one month in prison;
- In 1887, securities violations relating to transfer or issuance was a one-year prison sentence;
- In 1888, bribery of an inspector of Baltimore or New York harbors resulted in a six-month prison sentence;
- In 1888, refusal to operate railroad or telegraph lines brought a six-month sentence;
- In 1915, the unauthorized practice of pharmacy resulted in a one-month sentence;
- In 1948, treason and sedition was five years in prison;
- In 1965, first degree murder of a U.S. president or member of his staff was life in prison;
- In 1974, skyjacking resulted in 20 years in prison.

Congress Outdid Itself

So you can see how historically (and perhaps hysterically) Congress has responded to what it perceives the current major national threat, passing a mandatory prison sentence for it. But in the mid-1980s, Congress outdid itself. Between 1984 and 1990 members of Congress enacted four statutes that account for 94 percent of the cases sentenced under mandatory minimums. Those four statutes are for drug and gun offenses.

The laws were enacted with haste, without the benefit of hearings or any analysis of their likely impact. Grossly overcrowded prisons and race-based disparities in punishment have resulted. The new legislation was driven by another "crime du jour"—the cocaine overdose of University of Maryland basketball star Len Bias, and by the rise of crack cocaine. Congress passed laws sentencing defendants with a specific quantity of drugs to mandatory prison sentences of predetermined length, generally five or ten years without parole. No mitigating factors could be considered, and only the prosecutor would have the discretion to reduce the sentence based on his or her subjective determination that "substantial assistance" had been provided—that the accused had turned in others ripe for prosecution.

A Stunning Impact

The impact of these laws has been stunning. Not in any reduction of drug use, but in the denial of liberty to thousands of nonviolent drug offenders who now crowd our prisons. In 1986, when the majority of the drug mandatory minimums were passed, 38 percent of the federal prison population were drug offenders. [In 1998], that number is 60 percent. In 1998, 57 percent of drug defendants entering federal prison were first offenders, and 88 percent of them had no weapons.

We are not catching drug kingpins. We are catching the little guys, the girlfriends, the mules, and we are sending them to prison for 5 years, 10 years, and often much longer. And politicians largely don't give a damn. They don't care that we are destroying the lives of these defendants, labeling them forever "felons," removing them from their families, often leaving wives and children without a breadwinner.

"Dangerous Drug Offenders"

There are more than 133,000 people in federal prison today, and 80,000 of them are there for drug offenses. Their average sentence is 76 months—nearly 6.5 years behind bars. They are people like my brother, and Denese Calixte, a 51-year-old mother of seven when she was convicted of possession with intent to distribute crack cocaine and sentenced to 10 years in prison. Her offense? After falling from a ladder while picking fruit in Florida to support her family, Denese injured her neck and could no longer work. A man who sold small quantities of drugs in her neighborhood asked Denese if he could occasionally leave his drugs with her overnight, for which he would pay her $200 each night. The drugs were stored in a pill bottle or cigar tube (not exactly a kingpin quantity). Somehow the police found out and broke into Denese's house and found the drugs. She is still in prison.

Linda Lee Messer, who as a 45-year-old mother of three working as a housekeeper earning $6.50 an hour, was sentenced to five years in prison for manufacturing marijuana. The sheriff's department received a tip that there was marijuana growing on property belonging to Linda and her husband. When they searched the property, they found 184 seedlings and 1,000 grams of processed marijuana. The case was referred to the U.S. District Court and the jury deadlocked in Linda's first trial. She was found guilty in the second trial. At sentencing, Judge William Stafford of the U.S. District Court, Northern District of Florida, said: "These local matters, it seems to me, are dealt with better on a local level, or else the federal court becomes so trivialized that it no longer has room for the real important national cases."

Todd Davidson, who was 21 years old and following the Grateful Dead on tour when he was arrested in Florida for conspiracy to possess with intent to distribute LSD, was sent to federal prison. The circumstances surrounding his arrest and incarceration were remarkable. He and a fellow "Deadhead" were sharing a motel room where the fellow Deadhead had arranged for several LSD deals with undercover agents. When they busted him, Todd was arrested as well, even though he never participated in any of the deals. He is serving a 10-year sentence.

These are the "dangerous drug offenders" now filling America's federal prisons; they are just a few of the 400,000 drug defendants serving state and federal prison sentences across the land.

A Shameful Period

This is a shameful period in American history. I look forward to the day that we, as a nation, look back on this period with horror—wondering how we could have incarcerated so many nonviolent offenders for so many years.

We must repeal these mandatory minimum sentencing laws. That will not be drug-law reform, but it will be lifesaving. There are changes we can make today, that will immediately make a difference in the lives of people already sentenced, or those who will soon be sentenced.

[In 1999] in Michigan, FAMM succeeded in getting Michigan's heinous drug-lifer law changed to allow for parole after 15 years. It is an incremental change, but it meant immediate freedom for four nonviolent drug prisoners serving life sentences, and the possibility of freedom for 200 others.

In Congress, Rep. Maxine Waters (D-CA), has introduced legislation to repeal the mandatory minimum sentencing laws for drug offenders. Waters may not be some people's first choice for carrying the torch of sentencing reform, but she is the only member of Congress with the guts to do it, and we applaud her for it. More lawmakers need to take a stand for justice for the thousands of nonviolent drug offenders who are rotting in America's prisons.

"Drugs, alcohol, tobacco, peer pressure and other significant influences will always be present and any program that attempts to teach skills to resist these factors should be applauded."

The Drug Abuse Resistance Education Program Reduces Drug Use

Tim Schennum

Tim Schennum is a police officer in Costa Mesa, California, where he supervises the Drug Abuse Resistance Education (DARE) program. In the following viewpoint Schennum asserts that DARE teaches young students more than how to resist getting involved in drugs; it also teaches students skills to overcome peer pressure, how to avoid violence in various situations, and how to make proper decisions. Schennum admits that no program is 100 percent successful in keeping children away from drugs, but he contends that any program that tries to teach students to stay away from drugs, alcohol, and cigarettes should be applauded.

As you read, consider the following questions:

1. Which DARE programs have been revised, according to Schennum?
2. DARE is taught in how many school districts as cited by the author?
3. How long is the DARE program, according to Schennum?

Tim Schennum, "Unfair Rap for DARE," *Law and Order*, vol. 49, August 2001, p. 103. Copyright © 2001 by *Law and Order*. Reproduced by permission.

The editorial in the April 2001 issue of *Law and Order* was the most recent to address the perceived ineffectiveness of the Drug Abuse Resistance Education program. *Law and Order* is not the only one to jump on that bandwagon. The February 26, 2001, issue of *Newsweek* bashed the program in an article entitled, "DARE Checks Into Rehab." *Newsweek* only discussed one city that had chosen to discontinue its use of the DARE program, a decision that sounded more like a political move than a benefit for those parties involved.

Yes, it is true DARE America and the law enforcement community have taken a hard look at the existing DARE program. With the work from Ohio's Akron University, they have developed a revised curriculum for implementation at the junior high and high school level. However, the existing DARE program, specifically the grade school curriculum, has not been eliminated or changed.

To date, it has activated this new curriculum in cluster groups of schools in large cities across the country. The long-term plan is to conduct follow-up studies. A large part of the upcoming studies will be the evaluation of the new curriculum versus the old and the determination of impact each of them have on the future of the students who participated.

The unfortunate part of how some people have viewed the "old" DARE, and its impact with the youth of America, is that it only attempts to teach drug resistance. This could not be any further from the truth.

Let's set the stage with the background of DARE. Since 1983, two decades of hardworking, dedicated police officers have been spreading the DARE message. One excellent indicator of the knowledge these students have gained is through a select few essays that are read to the people in attendance.

Valuable Lessons Learned

After hearing these essays it is obvious the kids who participated were taught some valuable lessons and not just the pitfalls of getting involved in drugs. They were taught skills to overcome peer pressure; were given tools to make proper decisions; and were educated with alternatives to violence in various situations they may be presented with.

At present, it is refreshing to see DARE is still alive and effective. Today DARE is taught in more than 80% of all U.S. school districts, benefiting over 26 million students. DARE is an excellent program to assist parents and society as a whole in the fight against the influences of drugs, alcohol and tobacco on children and young adults.

DARE Works

Anita McKellar, president of the DARE Works! Society, visited the Foothills School Division [in Alberta, Canada].

According to survey results of Grade 6 students, parents, teachers and administrators, the DARE program has had a positive impact on the students and how they handle peer pressure.

McKellar reported that because of the program, there are fewer Grade 7 students smoking and a positive peer pressure to not smoke has developed.

What this indicates to the society, according to McKellar, is that "Children are learning these kinds of things and are carrying that over to the junior high level."

Cindy Ballance, *Westen Wheel*, February 27, 2002.

It is easy for some recent critics to sit back and Monday morning quarterback DARE and its effectiveness. But the reality is for every negative study launched against DARE, there are refuting studies to support DARE and how well it has done with informing kids about the evils that confront them. You can see this by simply driving through communities where DARE is taught, in areas wherever school age kids congregate. They will gravitate toward police cars as they stop on the neighborhoods streets; they look to socialize with officers.

They ask for badge stickers and baseball cards, and they want to view the police equipment. They are respectful and excited about the prospect of seeing an officer in their community.

The truth is that no program, formula, curriculum or course, no matter how wonderful, can ensure 100% effectiveness in preventing children from partaking in harmful acts. Dr. Donald R. Lynam, an apparent non-supporter of the

DARE Program, provided the following in an American Psychological Association release, dated August 1, 1999: "Although the DARE intervention produced a few initial improvements in the students' attitudes toward drug use, the researchers found that these changes did not persist over time." A few results are far better than none. This is probably true of many self-improvement programs; the effectiveness dissipates as time passes.

A Tried and True Program

DARE, however, is a tried and true program that has had some documented successes. Are they long term? Sure, in some cases. However, we may forever be faced with a fight, DARE or no DARE, particularly as our country moves towards the potential legalization of some drugs and the leniency toward sentencing offenders who possess narcotics for personal use. Drugs, alcohol, tobacco, peer pressure and other significant influences will always be present and any program that attempts to teach skills to resist these factors should be applauded.

Let's keep in mind that DARE, although a successful prospectus, is still just a 45 minute session, once a week, for 17 weeks. There are many hours when these impressionable minds are exposed to many of life's potential perils. It helps to have each child surrounded by peers and adults who will help to instill the proper values to keep them on the path of decency.

The new curriculum is welcomed with opened arms. Improvements that can be made, no matter how small, are important. We in law enforcement must change with our communities, by looking to improve all facets of our goals and objectives, or we would do an injustice to the communities we serve.

"America's most pervasive and expensive youth drug education program is (and always has been) a gigantic and incontrovertible flop."

The Drug Abuse Resistance Education Program Is Ineffective

Paul Armentano

The Drug Abuse Resistance Education (DARE) program fails to prevent students from using illegal drugs, argues Paul Armentano in the following viewpoint. According to Armentano, studies have found that students who have participated in the program show no significant difference in their attitudes toward illegal drugs compared to children who have not participated in DARE. Despite its failure to keep students off drugs, however, DARE remains a popular program in schools. Armentano believes that intensive lobbying by DARE officials fills the program's coffers with millions of dollars each year. Armentano is a senior policy analyst for the NORML Foundation in Washington, D.C., a non-profit lobbying organization working to legalize marijuana.

As you read, consider the following questions:

1. When was the DARE program established, and by whom, according to Armentano?
2. What two explanations do researchers for the APA give for why DARE continues to be popular in schools?

Paul Armentano, "The Truth About DARE," www.mises.org, March 31, 2003. Copyright © 2003 by the Ludwig Von Mises Institute, 518 West Magnolia Avenue, Auburn, AL 36832. Reproduced by permission.

If popularity was the sole measure of success then D.A.R.E., the "Drug Abuse Resistance Education" curriculum that is now taught in 80 percent of school districts nationwide, would be triumphant. However, if one is to gauge success by actual results, then America's most pervasive and expensive youth drug education program is (and always has been) a gigantic and incontrovertible flop.

So says the General Accounting Office (GAO) in a scathing . . . report that finds the politically popular program has had "no statistically significant long-term effect on preventing youth illicit drug use." In addition, students who participate in D.A.R.E. demonstrate "no significant differences . . . [in] attitudes toward illicit drug use [or] resistance to peer pressure" compared to children who had not been exposed to the program, the GAO determined.

Their critique was the latest in a long line of stinging evaluations that have plagued D.A.R.E. throughout its 20-year history. Established in 1983 by former Los Angeles police chief Daryl—All casual drug users should be taken out and shot!—Gates, the D.A.R.E. elementary school curriculum consists of 17 lessons—taught by D.A.R.E-trained uniform police officers—urging kids to resist the use of illicit drugs, including the underage use of alcohol and tobacco. Upon completion of the curriculum, which often relies on scare tactics and transparent "just say no" ideology, graduates "pledge to lead a drug-free life." Numerous studies indicate few do.

What the Studies Found

These include:
- A 1991 University of Kentucky study of 2,071 sixth graders that found no difference in the past-year use of cigarettes, alcohol or marijuana among DARE graduates and non-graduates two years after completing the program.
- A 1996 University of Colorado study of over 940 elementary school students that found no difference with regard to illicit drug use, delay of experimentation with illicit drugs, self-esteem, or resistance to peer pressure among D.A.R.E. graduates and non-graduates three years after completing the program.

DeBaTiNG CoNTiNUeD USe oF THe DaRE PROGRaM

Anderson. © 2001 by Kirk Anderson. Reprinted with permission.

- A 1998 University of Illinois study of 1,798 elementary school students that found no differences with regards to the recent use of illicit drugs among D.A.R.E. graduates and non-graduates six years after completing the program.
- A 1999 follow-up study by the University of Kentucky that found no difference in lifetime, past-year, or past-month use of marijuana among D.A.R.E. graduates and non-graduates 10 years after completing the program.

In fact, over the years so many studies have assailed D.A.R.E.'s effectiveness that by 2001 even its proponents admitted it needed serious revamping. However, rather than shelving the failed program altogether, D.A.R.E.'s advocates called for expanding its admittedly abysmal curriculum to target middle-school and high-school students—a move that was lauded by many federal officials and peer educators despite a track record that would spell the demise for most any other program.

So why does D.A.R.E. remain so immensely popular with politicians (Both [George H.W.] Bush and [Bill] Clinton endorsed "National D.A.R.E. Day.") and school administrators despite its stunning lack of demonstrated efficacy? Researchers writing in the American Psychological Association's *Journal of Consulting and Clinical Psychology* offer two explanations.

Explanations

The first is that for many civic leaders, teaching children to refrain from drugs simply "feels good." Therefore, advocates of the program perceive any scrutiny of their effectiveness to be overly critical and unnecessary.

The second explanation is that D.A.R.E. and similar youth anti-drug education programs appear to work. After all, most kids who graduate D.A.R.E. do not enage in drug use beyond the occasional beer or marijuana cigarette. However, this reality is hardly an endorsement of D.A.R.E., but an acknowledgement of the statistical fact that most teens—even without D.A.R.E.—never engage in any significant drug use.

Of course, those looking for a third explanation could simply follow the money trail. Even though D.A.R.E. has been a failure at persuading kids to steer away from drugs, it has been a marketing cash cow—filling its coffers with hundreds of millions of dollars in annual federal aid. (According to the GAO, exact totals are unavailable but outside experts have placed this figure at anywhere from $600 to $750 million per year.)

In addition, police departments spend an additional $215 million yearly on D.A.R.E. to pay for their officers' participation in the program, according to the *New York Times*. But this total may be only the tip of the iceberg. According to a preliminary economic assessment by Le Moyne College in New York, the total economic costs of officers' training and participation in D.A.R.E. is potentially closer to $600 million.

Regardless of its ultimate financial cost to taxpayers, there is no doubt that D.A.R.E. has become its own special interest group—aggressively lobbying state and federal governments to maintain its swelling budget. Like a junkie, D.A.R.E. is addicted to the money, and will do whatever it takes to get it. Meanwhile, its proponents remain in a state of denial, caring more about political posturing than embracing a youth drug education program that really works. After 20 years of failure, isn't it about time someone dares to tell the truth?

> *"Drug court graduates reoffend less often than other sentenced offenders and, when they do, their crimes are on average far less serious."*

Drug Courts Are a Promising Solution to the Drug Problem

Richard S. Gebelein

Drug courts aim to rehabilitate criminals guilty of minor drug offenses by combining treatment, testing, and judicial supervision in lieu of incarceration. According to Richard S. Gebelein in the following viewpoint, such courts were established in response to a dramatic escalation of drug cases beginning in the 1980s. Gebelein argues that drug courts have proved successful in rehabilitating minor drug offenders. However, he cautions that success rates are likely to fall as more varied criminals are entered into drug court programs. Gebelein is an associate judge in the Superior Court of Delaware and the founder of Delaware's Statewide Drug Court.

As you read, consider the following questions:

1. What percentage of Delaware's prisoners needed substance abuse treatment at the time the state's drug court program was being designed, according to Gebelein?
2. As reported by the author, what are Delaware's diversionary court requirements?
3. What specific successes has Delaware's drug court realized, according to the author?

Richard S. Gebelein, "The Rebirth of Rehabilitation: Promise and Perils of Drug Courts," *Sentencing & Corrections: Issues for the 21st Century*, May 2000. Copyright © 2000 by Richard S. Gebelein. Reproduced by permission.

D rug cases began to escalate dramatically in the 1980s. Petty drug offenders were recycling through the justice system at an alarming rate. Delaware's situation was typical. Overwhelmed with drug cases, the State's courts sought ways to manage case flow and solve the "revolving door" problem. Courts everywhere also sought sentencing alternatives for addicted offenders.

The situation brought to the fore questions about the link of substance abuse to crime. About this time, research was shedding better light on the issue. A study conducted in 1987 revealed that a large proportion of arrestees in several major urban areas tested positive for illegal substances. When the Delaware drug court was in the design stage, a study of the State's prisoners revealed that 80 percent needed substance abuse treatment. Researchers were also finding that when addicted offenders used drugs, they were among the most active perpetrators of other crimes.

At the same time, it was becoming established that if treatment reduced drug use by criminally involved addicts, it would also reduce their tendency to commit crime. Research was also proving that compelled treatment was as effective as voluntary treatment. Delaware would find, and other research would confirm, that in-prison treatment based on the therapeutic community (TC) model dramatically affects drug use and recidivism.

Drug Courts Emerge

All these factors converged to create a climate conducive to the growth of drug courts. When the National Association of Drug Court Professionals (NADCP) was established in 1994, the drug court judges who founded it numbered fewer than 15. Only 5 years later, the NADCP's annual training meeting drew 3,000 participants. About 10 years after Miami created what was arguably the first drug court, there were drug courts in almost every State and the District of Columbia. The expansion to more than 400 by the end of 1999 is evidence of the movement's popularity.

The movement gained wide acceptance for many of the reasons rehabilitation did in the 1950s. It offered hope of solving a grave problem. It is innovative, leveraging the court's power to compel drug-involved offenders to use a method that works—treatment. Its advantage over "plain old" rehabilitation is the focus on one problem (addiction) that is causally related to crime committed by one group of offenders (addicts). Treatment is reinforced with a healthy dose of specific deterrence as a motivation to achieve a specific result—abstinence. Federal legislation provided an added impetus, as the 1994 Crime Act provided funding to establish or expand drug courts.

The nature, structure, and jurisdiction of drug courts vary widely. Given the many variations, it became important to achieve consensus on what is a "true" drug court. The NADCP and the U.S. Department of Justice identified the following key elements:

- Integration of substance abuse treatment with justice system case processing.
- Use of a nonadversarial approach, in which prosecution and defense promote public safety while protecting the right of the accused to due process.
- Early identification and prompt placement of eligible participants.
- Access to a continuum of treatment, rehabilitation, and related services.
- Frequent testing for alcohol and illicit drugs.
- A coordinated strategy among judge, prosecution, defense, and treatment providers to govern offender compliance.
- Ongoing judicial interaction with each participant.
- Monitoring and evaluation to measure achievement of program goals and gauge effectiveness.
- Continuing interdisciplinary education to promote effective planning, implementation, and operation.
- Partnerships with public agencies and community-based organizations to generate local support and enhance drug court effectiveness.

Most drug courts attempt to integrate these components. One reason is that Federal funding is contingent on a plan that incorporates them all.

In general, the offender enters the program through a plea, conditional plea, contract with the court, or similar mechanism. The offender is assigned to a treatment program and told when to report to court. Court appearances can be as frequent as several times a week or can be once a month or less often. Urinalysis is frequent and usually on a random basis. Urinalysis positives or missed treatments or court appointments result in immediate sanctions. In Delaware's diversionary court, requirements include 4 months of total abstinence in addition to holding a steady job, successfully completing treatment, earning a general equivalency diploma if applicable, participating in 12-step meetings, developing a support network, and maintaining a stable residence.

Drug Courts Are Cost-Effective

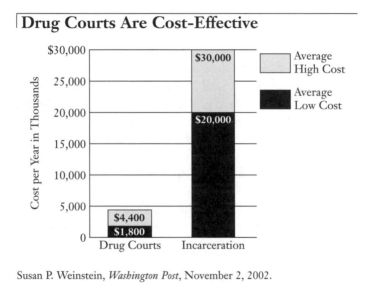

Susan P. Weinstein, *Washington Post*, November 2, 2002.

The first drug courts dealt primarily with minor drug offenses, with offenders placed on a diversionary or quasi-diversionary track. Newer designs include postadjudicative drug courts (those in which the offender is sentenced to drug court after conviction), juvenile drug courts, and family drug courts. In the model most commonly used today, the population of substance-abusing offenders is wider and more varied than that of the first drug courts. Drug courts funded by the 1994 Crime Act may process only nonviolent offenders, but many drug courts that are wholly State funded or locally funded accept some violent offenders.

Delaware's drug courts in many respects typify drug courts in general. They began with an effort to solve the problem of drugs and crime. The State's Drug Involved Offender Coordination Committee, organized in 1991 to weigh proposed solutions, discovered flaws in the State's approach to offender substance abuse. Many court orders referring defendants to treatment were ignored by corrections officials. Related problems came to light. Offenders were more likely than non-court-referred participants to be discharged from treatment programs. Jail- or prison-based treatment was limited; there was no coordination between treatment in jail and the community; and treatment was inefficiently delivered and inadequate in relation to the need.

A treatment continuum did not exist. To create one, the Treatment Access Committee (TAC) was established and charged with ensuring that substance-abusing offenders did not "fall through the cracks."

Offenders

Delaware's potential treatment population was so large that only two groups could be targeted. Younger offenders, who are less criminally involved and who can possibly be diverted from a life of crime, were selected as one group.

The diversion track calls for a modest "investment" of 6 months to a year in drug court, with outpatient treatment and frequent urine tests. These offenders are not under sentence, so they are not supervised by probation. This saves resources, which can be used to supervise more serious offenders. However, offenders on this track are more accountable than those on regular probation. If the offender cannot stay drug free or otherwise fails, diversion is terminated, a trial is held, and, if it results in conviction, the usual sentence is probation with compelled treatment. If all conditions are met, the offender graduates and the charge is dismissed.

Offenders in jail or prison because of violating probation were another group identified as needing substantial investment of treatment resources. TAC felt that a drug court model could work with them, although outpatient treatment without probation supervision was unlikely to work with many. This group of more serious offenders consists largely of people convicted of 6 to 10 felonies and addicted for 12 to 20 years.

The probation revocation model is for offenders charged with a new crime. The prosecutor offers to resolve the new offense and the probation violation simultaneously, through a plea and an "addiction sentence" that always includes drug court–supervised treatment. If the defendant accepts the offer, he or she is immediately sentenced on both counts. If the defendant is sentenced to jail or prison, he or she enters a treatment program in the correctional facility. Successful completion means the remaining prison time is suspended and replaced with supervision and treatment in the community. The addiction sentence allows the court to require this treatment continuum through the in-prison "Key" program, followed by work release and continued treatment in the "Crest" program and aftercare in the community. In effect, the model provides for indeterminate sentencing—tailored to the offender, with the goal of rehabilitation—in a truth-in-sentencing State.

All addiction sentences require frequent court appearances, and the assignment of a Treatment Alternatives to Street Crime (TASC) case manager, to ensure continuum of treatment in the transition from jail to halfway house to community. Failure in this track usually results in a prison sentence with an order to participate in a long-term therapeutic community while incarcerated, followed again by treatment in the community, with reentry monitored by the drug court.

Drug Courts Prove Effective

Scientifically based evaluations of Delaware's drug courts are not completed, but initial studies are encouraging. The figures on numbers of diversion track graduates are a rough estimate: By the end of 1999, charges were dismissed for 2,670 people—about half of those who entered the program. Case studies demonstrate that the lives of people once considered total criminal justice failures have been saved. The widespread belief among judges, prosecutors, defense attorneys, and others that the Delaware drug courts are working and turning lives around cannot easily be discounted.

Treatment providers indicated 18 months into the program that their drug court clients are more likely to complete treatment than are their other clients, and that they stay in treatment longer. Preliminary evaluation results suggest that Delaware drug court graduates reoffend less often than other sentenced offenders and, when they do, their crimes are on average far less serious. Studies of drug courts in other jurisdictions offer similarly encouraging findings. The past 3 years' experience in Delaware indicates that offenders adjudicated through the probation revocation track spend less time in prison than do other offenders sentenced for similar crimes. This is because drug court offenders can earn early release by completing treatment.

Drug courts will not solve the drug problem or eliminate crime in Delaware or anywhere else. But if they offer a comprehensive treatment continuum, solid case management, and meaningful immediate sanctions, they can have a major effect on public safety. They are a powerful tool for addressing the criminal behavior of people who commit disproportionately large numbers of crimes. . . .

Possible Perils

The drug court movement is currently riding a wave of success. Initial evaluations are favorable. New courts are being established everywhere. The movement is supported by both major political parties and the news media. Even more important, it has captured the imagination of the public. Ironically, success is perhaps the biggest peril drug courts face.

Success with a narrowly defined offender population does not translate into a universal solution to drug crime.

As the results of more sophisticated evaluations become available, preliminary success rates will not be sustained. As less tractable groups participate, rates of compliance and graduation will decline and recidivism will rise. Support may fade as success appears to diminish. The movement cannot afford to claim too much and so must define success realistically.

Differences in treatment options and in groups that participate will affect outcomes. Some drug courts, such as Delaware's probation revocation track, include a full spectrum of treatment options. Others, such as Delaware's diversion track, rely primarily on outpatient treatment, drug education, and urine tests. Success is likely to vary with the treatment available.

In Delaware's probation revocation track, the participants are far more involved with drugs and other crime than those on the diversion track, who are younger, are less severely addicted, and have less extensive criminal histories. Different success rates can be expected from the different populations.

In identifying target populations, drug courts need to be sensitive to class and race bias, real or apparent. Unless care is taken, diversion courts may tend disproportionately to work with white and middle-class substance abusers. In Delaware, the client demographics of the diversion and probation revocation tracks were at first virtual opposites. Participants in the latter were disproportionately minority group members from disadvantaged backgrounds; those in the former were more likely to be white and middle class. Delaware has aggressively addressed this imbalance.

Differences in populations and treatments can lead to the same problems that came to light in research on boot camps. Initially, boot camps were highly popular (perhaps for all the wrong reasons). They proliferated quickly, and claims of success abounded. However, evaluations generally revealed that boot camps do little to reduce recidivism. As a result, funding eroded, fewer resources were allocated, and support all but evaporated. The same fate could befall drug courts if evaluations of individual courts that offer incomplete treatment or no real treatment at all reveal low success rates. . . .

Quick Solutions Will Fail

Americans want quick, decisive solutions. This is evident in the very terminology used for this national propensity: We wage a "War on Drugs." Yet as General Barry McCaffrey, [former] head of the Office of National Drug Control Policy, has noted, the problem cannot be solved this way. War requires concentrated maximum force at a critical point. For the drug problem, there is no silver bullet, nor is there a single program, model, or method that will eliminate either addiction or crime.

Because drug courts are effective in helping address one correlate of crime, they may also serve as a model to help address others. Research may reveal whether this expectation is realistic by demonstrating why drug courts work and whether similar principles are likely to work for groups other than drug-involved offenders. Delaware's proposed reentry court for nonaddicted offenders is an example of the extension of the model.

Judges tend to deal more often with failure than success. Many drug court judges, enthusiastic about their perceived successes, may yield to the temptation to claim they have the key to winning the war on drugs and criminal behavior. That claim will surely fail to be sustained. Instances of failure of the drug court method will become more widely reported. The movement's claims will be tested against results. If the claims of judges and others are unreasonably optimistic and not based in reality, backlash is inevitable.

The drug court movement focused initially on adult drug offenders who had histories of nonviolent offenses. Depending on the site, the movement now encompasses offenders convicted of several felonies, many of whom have criminal histories that qualify them for habitual offender status. The movement also extends to specialty courts dedicated to juvenile offending, domestic violence, and family issues and has fostered establishment of treatment courts for DUI cases.

There are other areas where the drug court approach may be useful. An example is "therapeutic jurisprudence," a new, problem-solving orientation adopted by some judges, courts, and court systems. Participants in the drug court movement believe that success is due in large part to direct judicial involvement with offenders, provided on a regular basis. It is likely that judges who have been successful with the approach will want to apply it to other areas.

In expanding the drug court model to clients other than drug users, care must be taken until more is known about why the process works and with what types of offenders it might be effective. That means first designing pilot programs, implementing them, and evaluating them. Drug courts hold great promise as a tool to prevent crime in the long term. For that to become reality, every effort must be taken to avoid the many perils that could make the movement just another failed criminal justice fad.

"There are many who are starting to question whether or not the drug court movement is the panacea of good will everyone says it is."

Drug Courts Have Not Reduced the Drug Problem

Melissa Hostetler

In the following viewpoint Melissa Hostetler contends that drug courts—which seek to rehabilitate criminals charged with minor drug offenses utilizing a combination of treatment, testing, and judicial supervision—are not as effective as many supporters claim. In fact, she argues, drug courts have not resulted in fewer people sentenced to prison for drug possession. Hostetler also asserts that drug courts are proving more expensive than incarceration, and she criticizes drug courts for using up the resources of community-based treatment programs, leaving many of those seeking voluntary drug treatment without help. Hostetler is a journalist and cofounder of Frictionmagazine.com.

As you read, consider the following questions:

1. How much money has the federal government spent on drug court programs since 1995, as reported by Hostetler?
2. According to the author, what has happened to the number of drug filings two years into Denver's drug court program?
3. What criticisms do some experts have about the judiciary's role in drug court programs?

Welcome to the San Francisco County drug court, just one of nearly a thousand courts in the country and one of more than a hundred in California alone offering drug treatment over incarceration. The court begins to come alive as the defendants—or clients as drug court professionals like to call them—arrive and speak in hushed tones with their counselors and attorneys.

In the hall, a counselor hugs a client twice her size and encourages him to stay with the treatment program. The client is later sent to jail on Judge Julie Tang's order for testing positive for drugs. Though this weekend-long prison stay is only considered a sanction, this client may very well end up in jail long-term.

A female clad in an orange jumper sits and watches as a half dozen soon to be ex-clients tell their story of how treatment and a second chance has changed their lives. As a new drug court recruit, she hears about their new jobs, new lives, and a new outlook on staying sober. She decides drug court is for her—the freedom of a probation-style life, the allure of having all charges dropped upon completion of the program, and the hope of finally being rid of the drug addiction disease seem all too convincing.

Examining Drug Courts

And though the argument for treatment-based drug courts seems convincing—the media are sold on the idea of treatment over prison, and the drug court movement is picking up steam as politicians who strive to be tough on crime and compassionate in one swoop are singing its praises—there are many who are starting to question whether or not the drug court movement is the panacea of good will everyone says it is.

Since the first treatment-based program was founded in Miami, Florida, [in the early 1990s,] the drug court epidemic has spread to nearly every state, adding up to more than 800 drug courts nationwide either operating or in the planning stages. US federal funding for the program now totals more than $80 million since 1995 in a political phenomenon that is getting support from all sides. Actor Martin Sheen, former Drug Czar Barry McCaffrey, and [former] Attorney General Janet Reno (who helped found the Florida drug court when she was Florida Attorney General) have lined up behind the program.

They call them the elixir to cure prison overcrowding, the cycling of drug offenders in and out of the criminal justice system, and the skyrocketing price-tag of the US prison system. In a closer look though, many have found that drug courts not only don't accomplish their goals but they may be widening the criminal justice net, increasing costs to the system, taking treatment slots away from voluntary, community-based programs, and blurring the traditional roles of judges, prosecutors, and defense attorneys.

"Drug courts are just the latest Band-Aid we have tried to apply over the deep wound of our schizophrenia about drugs," says Denver, Colorado, Judge Morris B. Hoffman in a *North Carolina Law* review article that is one of the few critical pieces on drug courts. "Drug courts themselves have become a kind of institutional narcotic upon which the entire criminal justice system is becoming increasingly dependent."

Though they are designed to relieve the criminal justice system of some of its burden—one in four American prisoners is incarcerated for a non-violent drug offense—drug courts may actually be increasing the number of people brought into the system and thus also negating most of their expected savings.

"What we've started to see happening is people who previously would have essentially not been arrested at all or given a short term of probation or a fine wound up getting arrested," says Katherine Huffman of the Lindesmith Center for Drug Policy Foundation.

Increases in Drug Arrests

In Denver, drug filings tripled just two years into the drug court program. Not only had the number tripled, but the percentage of drug filings went from 30 percent of all filings to 52 percent in that same period.

California, home to more than 100 drug courts, also saw drug arrests for possession only offenses increase from 40 percent of all drug arrests to 53 percent in the past ten years. It is not clear though what effect if any drug courts have made directly.

"All we know is that drug courts have not resulted in fewer people sentenced to prison for drug possession offenses in California," says Dan Macalair of the Justice Policy Institute. "In fact, the evidence is just the opposite."

The increased arrests, says Jeff Tauber, president of the National Association of Drug Court Professionals, is that the justice system has chosen to start dealing with those previously ignored. By bringing offenders into the system early on, drug courts can avoid repeated offenses, he says.

A survey suggests, though, that law enforcement see drug courts as a solution to America's drug problems. Two-thirds of the 300 police chiefs polled in a survey do not want to cut federal drug court funding, and 60 percent claim drug courts are more effective than prison or jail time.

"The very presence of the drug court has caused police to make arrests in, and prosecutors to file, the kinds of ten- and twenty-dollar hand-to-hand drug cases that the system simply would not have bothered with before, certainly not as felonies," says Judge Hoffman.

Drug Courts Cost More

With the increased number of drug offenders coming into the criminal justice system, the cost savings promised by drug courts are largely non-existent. According to the Vera Institute of Justice, many cost-savings analyses fail to account for common drug court practices that ultimately erode savings—detaining offenders for detoxification and punishing non-compliant participants with jail time. When interim jail stays are counted, drug court participants could spend more time in jail than if they had simply been sentenced. The Vera Institute also found evidence to suggest that participants who fail in drug court may be sentenced more harshly than those never entering a drug court.

The problem though with determining whether or not drug courts are actually working is in the research itself.

For example, drug courts claim to reduce the cycle of drug offenders coming in and out of the prison system. The Department of Justice's Drug Courts Program Office claims a reduction in recidivism between five and 28 percent, but not all studies show these results. An Arizona drug court study found no difference in recidivism between those in standard probation and those in drug court. Another evaluation of 21 drug courts found that five could not claim they reduced recidivism.

The problem says Judge Hoffman is the method of evaluation. Drug court professionals who have a vested interest in continuing the program are often the ones doing the drug court impact studies, resulting in what is little more than a morale booster for drug court professionals.

The very nature of localized drug courts allows for survey results that cannot be compared. Without a comprehensive data source, there is no telling how well the drug court program is actually working, says Macalair. Not to mention, he adds, the surveys themselves do not seem to be asking the right questions—for example, true cost analyses of drug court treatment programs have seldom been done.

Tauber says the results are not solely in speculated recidivism improvements. Retention, he says, is the defining factor of how well the program is working, citing that drug courts keep people in treatment longer making it more likely they will stick to their new lifestyle.

Taking Resources from Voluntary Treatment Programs

But on top of these woes are the concerns for the larger picture of drug treatment in America.

Most who question the drug court strategy prefer treatment to incarceration, but would rather see resources put into voluntary treatment and court-mandated treatment. But instead of creating new slots to answer the call of the thousands waiting for treatment, drug courts are absorbing some of these treatment slots, says Graham Boyd, director of the ACLU Drug Litigation Project.

Drug courts have flourished largely because of the enormous political support given them. But there is no such will for adding more community-based treatment, leaving the system skewed in favor of the criminal justice system at the cost of voluntary treatment, says Daniel Abrahamson, director of legal affairs for the Lindesmith Center.

It's logical to want to treat everyone, Tauber says, but the motivation and consequences of drug court are much stronger and tangible for addicts to complete the program and get off drugs than if they entered treatment on their own. In fact, Tauber says drug courts provide better results than voluntary treatment because they tend to keep addicts in treatment longer.

Changing Attitudes Toward the Criminal Justice System

Asked whether drug abuse should be addressed primarily through counseling and treatment or through the criminal justice system, 63 percent of Americans believe counseling and treatment is the most effective method.

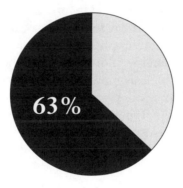

Drug Policy Alliance, "Reducing Harm: Treatment and Beyond," 2002.

But even if drug courts are working, their essential nature runs contrary to the traditional roles of the justice system. That, say critics, is not only bad for drug court defendants but for the public as well.

An Unrestrained Judiciary

This non-adversarial nature found in drug courts—where the judge, the prosecutor, and the defense attorney are all working toward the uniform goal of keeping the defendant in treatment—is precisely why drug courts work, say drug court professionals. Drug court judges are able to exercise a fair amount of discretion, thus making the system more tailored for each individual. The drug court system though allows judges to become social workers and pseudo-doctors, and critics say this is not the type of discretion that the criminal justice system needs or deserves. The judicial branch, they say, is not the arena for handling what is essentially a public policy issue.

"The real problem with the drug courts is that the judges don't know what treatment is," says Dr. John McCarthy, a psychiatrist and addiction medicine specialist at the Bi-Valley Medical Clinic in Sacramento. Judges aren't doctors, he says, and the drug court structure makes "every judge his own king."

Though in some jurisdictions treatment professionals are in the court to directly advise a judge on what to do, the judge ultimately gets to make the final decisions.

"I cannot imagine a more dangerous branch than an unrestrained judiciary full of amateur psychiatrists poised to 'do good' rather than to apply the law," says Judge Hoffman.

The drug court method, in fact, is just the first sample of what may come if the problem-solving court model spreads to the arenas of domestic violence, mental health, and prostitution as many like Tauber hope it will. To function, these courts will need these non-traditional roles and judges willing to institute them, says San Francisco Superior Court Judge Julie Tang.

"In other courts, the outcome is punishment and rehabilitation if necessary," she says. "In our case it's rehabilitation as the goal and purpose of the court. You need to have a different structure to produce outcomes."

Though the idea may be a noble and humane one—helping people and keeping them out of prison—critics say it is wrong to treat these problems as diseases and then punish offenders in a system where no one is working for the offenders themselves. And in a system that is being exported across borders—Canada's federal government has plans to set up drug courts in every major city by 2004—this, critics say, could end in a strange downward spiral where the judicial system serves the welfare state and no one serves the law or the people.

Periodical Bibliography

The following articles have been selected to supplement the diverse views presented in this chapter.

American Civil Liberties Union	"Drug Testing in the Workplace," 1996. www.aclu.org.
Robert Batey	"Mandatory Minimum Sentencing: A Failed Policy," *Phi Kappa Phi Forum*, Winter 2002.
Mark Boal	"The Supreme Court vs. Teens," *Rolling Stone*, June 6, 2002.
Fox Butterfield	"New Drug-Offender Program Draws Unexpected Clients," *New York Times*, September 29, 2001.
Joseph A. Califano Jr.	"A Turning Point on Drugs," *Washington Post*, March 13, 2001.
Peter Cassidy	"Pee First, Ask Questions Later," *In These Times*, December 20, 2002.
Eric Cohen	"The Drug Court Revolution," *Weekly Standard*, December 27, 1999.
James Emery	"Thailand's World-Class Antidrug Program, *World and I*, February 2003.
John Gould	"Zone Defense: Drug-Free School Zones Were Supposed to Keep Dealers Away from Kids," *Washington Monthly*, June 2002.
Todd Hutlock	"Addressing Concerns About Drug Courts," *Behavioral Health Management*, March/April 2003.
Walter Kirn	"Hidden Lessons," *New York Times Magazine*, April 14, 2002.
Eric D. Lock, Jeffrey M. Timberlake, and Kenneth A. Rasinski	"Battle Fatigue: Is Public Support Waning for 'War'-Centered Drug Control Strategies?" *Crime and Delinquency*, July 2002.
Ken MacQueen	"Getting Addicts off the Streets," *Maclean's*, March 17, 2003.
David Masci	"Preventing Teen Drug Use: Is the 'Get-Tough' Approach Effective?" *CQ Researcher*, March 15, 2002.
Ed Sanow	"Old Problem, New DARE," *Law and Order*, April 2001.
Jacob Sullum	"Constant Improvement," *Reason*, November 2002.
Jacob Sullum	"Free Will," *Reason*, May 2002.
Sanho Tree	"The War at Home," *Sojourners*, May/June 2003.

CHAPTER 4

Should Illegal Drugs Be Legalized?

Chapter Preface

In 1997 the White House Office of National Drug Control Policy asked the Institute of Medicine (IOM) to study the scientific literature on marijuana used for medicinal purposes and determine whether the drug had any health benefits. Two years later, Janet E. Joy, Stanley J. Watson Jr., and John A. Benson released their report, *Marijuana and Medicine: Assessing the Science Base*. In their report the authors examined and evaluated marijuana's effects on the human body and the risks associated with the medical use of marijuana. Both supporters and opponents of medical marijuana have found conclusions in the report they can use to support their arguments.

Supporters of legalizing marijuana for medicinal purposes cite several sections of the report in which Joy, Watson, and Benson report that marijuana can relieve pain, control nausea, stimulate the appetite, reduce anxiety, and act as a sedative. The authors of the report also recommend that more research be performed to evaluate the drug's physiological effects and to develop safe delivery methods. Supporters also note that Joy, Watson, and Benson refute the "gateway" theory, asserting that there is no "conclusive evidence that the drug effects of marijuana are causally linked to the subsequent abuse of other illicit drugs."

According to opponents of legalized medical marijuana, the report concedes that there are risks associated with using marijuana, the most serious of which are the effects of chronic marijuana smoking on the patient. Marijuana smoke is "an important risk factor in the development of respiratory disease," Joy, Watson, and Benson write. The researchers also found that a few users may become dependent on marijuana and experience withdrawal symptoms if the drug is withheld.

The fact that both supporters and opponents of legalized marijuana can use the same report to buttress their arguments shows how difficult it can be to formulate drug policies. The authors in the following chapter continue the debate over whether the benefits of legalizing drugs outweigh the risks involved.

> *"Legal prescription drugs are harder to come by than illegal drugs. . . . To get legal drugs, you must walk into a pharmacy and show identification. It's the difference between a controlled substance and an illegal substance."*

Illegal Drugs Should Be Legalized

Gary E. Johnson

Gary E. Johnson is the former governor of New Mexico. In the following viewpoint Johnson contends that the war on drugs has failed—even after spending billions of dollars on the war, millions of Americans still use illegal drugs. He maintains that if drugs are legalized, drug use will hold steady or decline. In addition, if drugs are legalized, the government can control, regulate, and tax them. According to Johnson, if drugs are legalized, the money spent on the war on drugs could then be redirected toward fighting crime and enforcing new drug laws.

As you read, consider the following questions:
1. How does Johnson characterize drugs and drug use?
2. If drugs are legalized, what are a few of the new laws Johnson proposes to regulate the sale and use of drugs?
3. How does Johnson respond to Drug Czar Barry McCaffrey's claim that drug use has been cut in half due to the war on drugs?

I am a cost-benefit analysis person. What's the cost and what's the benefit? A couple of things scream out as failing cost-benefit criteria. One is education. The other is the war on drugs. We are presently spending $50 billion a year on the war on drugs. I'm talking about police, courts, and jails. For all the money that we're putting into the war on drugs, it is an absolute failure. The "outrageous" hypothesis that I have been raising is that under a legalized scenario, we could actually hold drug use level or see it decline. I realize that is arguable. But with respect to drug abuse, I don't think you can argue about that. Under a legalized scenario, we would see the level of drug use remain the same or decline. And the same would happen with respect to drug abuse.

Sometimes people say to me, "Governor, I am absolutely opposed to your stand on drugs." I respond by asking them, "You're for drugs, you want to see kids use drugs?" Let me make something clear. I'm not pro-drug. I'm against drugs. Don't do drugs. Drugs are a real handicap. Don't do alcohol. Don't do tobacco. They are a real handicap.

A Legalized Scenario

There's another issue beyond cost-benefit criteria. Should you go to jail for using drugs? And I'm not talking about doing drugs and committing a crime or doing drugs and driving a car. Should you go to jail for simply doing drugs? I say no. I say that you shouldn't. People ask me, "What do you tell kids?" Well, you tell them the truth, that's what you tell them. You tell them that by legalizing drugs, we can control them, regulate them, and tax them. If we legalize drugs, we might have a healthier society. And you explain to them how that might take place. But you tell them that drugs are a bad choice. Don't do drugs. But if you do drugs, we're not going to throw you in jail for that.

Under a legalized scenario, I say there is going to be a whole new set of laws. Let me just mention a few of those new laws. Let's say you can't do drugs if you're under 21 years of age. You can't sell drugs to kids. I say employers should be able to discriminate against drug users. Employers should be able to conduct drug tests and they should not have to comply with the Americans With Disabilities Act.

Do drugs and do crime? Make it like a gun. Enhance the penalty for the crime in the same way we do today with guns. Do drugs and drive? There should be a law similar to the law we have now for driving under the influence of alcohol.

Enforce Other Laws

I am proposing that we redirect the $50 billion that we're presently spending (state and federal) on the old set of laws to enforce a new set of laws. I sense a new society out there when you're talking about enforcing these new laws and enhancing the ability of law enforcement to focus on other crimes that are being committed. Police can crack down on speeding violations, burglaries, and other crimes that law enforcement does not have the opportunity to enforce.

Under a legalized scenario, there will be a new set of problems. And we can all point them out. We can talk all day about the new set of problems that will accompany legalization. But I suggest to you that the new problems are going to be about half the negative consequence of what we've got today. A legalization model will be a dynamic process that will be fine-tuned as we go along.

Punishment

I recall when I was in high school in 1971. An Albuquerque police officer came in, lit up some marijuana weeds and said, "If you smell this, run. This is marijuana and you need to know that if you do marijuana, we're going to catch you and we're going to put you in jail." I remember raising my hand at that time, asking, "What are you going to do, put 15 million people in jail?" The police officer said, "I don't care about that. I just care about the fact that if you do it, we're going to catch you and we're going to put you in jail." I'm afraid that prophecy may be coming true. In 1997 there were about 700,000 arrests for marijuana-related offenses.

Does anybody want to press a button that would retroactively punish the 80 million Americans who have done illegal drugs over the years? I might point out that I'm one of those individuals. In running for my first term in office, I offered up the fact that I had smoked marijuana. And the media was very quick to say, "Oh, so you experimented with

146

marijuana?" "No," I said, "I *smoked* marijuana!" This is something that I did. I did it along with a lot of other people. I look back on it now and I view drugs as a handicap. I stopped because it was a handicap. The same with drinking and tobacco. But did my friends and I belong in jail? I don't think that we should continue to lock up Americans because of bad choices.

Alcohol and Tobacco

And what about the bad choices regarding alcohol and tobacco? I've heard people say, "Governor, you're not comparing alcohol to drugs? You're not comparing tobacco to drugs?" I say, *"Hell no!"* Alcohol killed 150,000 people [in 1999]. And I'm not talking about drinking and driving. I'm just talking about the health effects. The health effects of tobacco killed 450,000 people [in 1999]. I don't mean to be flippant, but I don't know of anybody who ever died from a marijuana overdose. I'm sure there are a few that smoked enough marijuana to probably die from it. I'm sure that that's the case. I understand that 2,000 to 3,000 people died last year from cocaine and heroin. Under a legalized scenario, theoretically speaking, those deaths go away. Those don't become accidental deaths anymore. They become suicides, because we'd be talking about a legalized scenario where drugs will be controlled, where drugs will be taxed, where we would have education to go along with it. I want to be so bold as to say that marijuana is never going to have the devastating effects on society that alcohol has had on us.

My own informal poll among doctors is that 75 to 80 percent of people that doctors examine have health-related problems due to alcohol and tobacco. My brother is a cardio-thoracic surgeon, performing heart transplants. My brother says that 80 percent of the problems that he sees are alcohol and tobacco related. He says he sees about six people a year who have infected heart valves because of intravenous drug use, but the infection isn't from the drugs themselves. It's the dirty needles that cause the health problems.

Marijuana is said to be a gateway drug. We all know that, right? You're 85 times more likely to do cocaine if you do marijuana. I don't mean to be flippant, but 100 percent of all substance abuse starts with milk. You've heard it, but that bears repeating. My new mantra here is "Just Say Know." Just know that there are two sides to all these arguments. I think the facts boil down to drugs being a bad choice. Drugs are a handicap. But should someone go to jail for just doing drugs? That is the reality of what is happening today. I believe the time has come for that to end.

A Controlled Substance

I've been talking about legalization and not decriminalization. Legalization means we educate, regulate, tax, and control the estimated $400 billion a year drug industry. That's larger than the automobile industry. Decriminalization is a muddy term. It turns its back to half the problems that we're facing—which is to get the entire economy of drugs above the line. So that's why I talk about legalization, meaning control, the ability to tax, the ability to regulate, and the ability to educate.

We need to make drugs a controlled substance just like alcohol. Perhaps we ought to let the government regulate it; let the government grow it; let the government manufacture it, distribute it, market it; and if that doesn't lead to decreased drug use, I don't know what would!

Kids today will tell you that legal prescription drugs are harder to come by than illegal drugs. Well, of course. To get legal drugs, you must walk into a pharmacy and show identification. It's the difference between a controlled substance and an illegal substance. A teenager today will tell you that a bottle of beer is harder to come by than a marijuana joint. That's where we've come to today. It's where we've come to with regard to controlling alcohol, but it shows how out of control drugs have become.

A legalization scenario isn't going to be like the end of alcohol prohibition. When Prohibition ended, there were advertisements on the radio right away that said, "Hey! Drink and be merry. It's cool." I don't see this like tobacco, where for so long we saw advertisements that said, "Hey! Smoking is good for your health." There are constitutional questions, but I envision advertising campaigns that discourage drug use. I don't see today's advertising campaigns as being honest, and that's part of the problem.

An Educational Campaign

We need to have an honest educational campaign about drugs. The Partnership for a Drug Free America was bragging to me that it was responsible for the "Here's your brain, and here's your brain on drugs" ad. Well, some kids believe that, perhaps three-year-olds, maybe some nine- or ten-year-olds. But at some point, kids have friends that smoke marijuana for the first time. Like everybody else, I was also told that if you smoke marijuana, you're going to go crazy. You're going to do crime. You're going to lose your mind. Then you smoked marijuana for the first time and none of those things happened. Actually, it was kind of nice. And then you realized that they weren't telling you the truth. That's why I envision advertising that tells the truth, which says drugs are kind of nice and that's the lure of drugs. But the reality is that if you continue to do drugs, they are a real handicap.

People Can Be Trusted

The case for repealing drug prohibition is based on two main propositions: that it does more harm than good, and that it violates the fundamental right to control one's body and mind. It is possible to hold either or both of these views and still condemn drug use on moral grounds. Indeed, the conventional wisdom among reformers is that defending the morality of drug use needlessly antagonizes those who might otherwise be inclined to agree that the war on drugs is counterproductive and unjust. That is why you will often hear ritual denunciations of drug use in seemingly unlikely places such as the Cato Institute. But the repeal of alcohol prohibition would have been impossible if most Americans did not recognize that people, by and large, can be trusted to drink responsibly. A successful campaign to end the war on drugs will also depend upon a belief in the possibility of temperance.

Jacob Sullum, *National Review Online*, February 22, 2001.

"Drug Czar" Barry McCaffrey has made me his poster child for drug legalization. He claims that drug use has been cut in half and that we are winning the drug war. Well, let's assume that we have cut it in half. I don't buy that for a minute, but let's assume that it's true. Let's assume that drug use has, in fact, dropped in half. Well, if it has, in the late

1970s we were spending a billion dollars federally on the drug war. Today, the feds are spending $19 billion a year on the drug war. In the late 1970s, we were arresting a few hundred thousand people. Today, we're arresting 1.6 million people. Does that mean that as drug use declines (according to McCaffrey, it has declined by half) we're going to be spending $36 billion federally and that we're going to be arresting 3.2 million people annually? I mean, to follow that logic, when we're left with a few hundred users nationwide, we're going to be spending the entire gross national product on drug law enforcement!

I think it would be interesting to see some push polling done on the issue of drugs in this country. In other words, if the following is true, then how do you feel about "x"? If the following is true, how do you feel about "y"? But the questions that get asked today, I really feel like I understand the answers. People have been conditioned to believe that drugs are dangerous. The polls should ask, "Should you go to jail for just using drugs?" People overwhelmingly say no. But ask the question, "Should you go to jail for pushing drugs?" people say yes. People don't understand the profile of a pusher. Most people don't understand, as we New Mexicans do, that "mules" are carrying the drugs in. I'm talking about Mexican citizens who are paid a couple of hundred dollars to bring drugs across the border, and they don't even know who has given them the money. They just know that it's a king's ransom and that there are more than enough Mexican citizens willing to do that. The federal government is catching many of the mules, but the arrests are not making a difference in our war on drugs. We are catching some kingpins. Let's not deny that. But those that are caught, those links out of the chain, don't make any difference in the overall war on drugs.

Public Response

I want to tell you a little bit about the response that I've been getting to this, the response to what I've been saying. Politically, this is a zero. This is absolutely a zero. Politically, for anybody holding office, for anybody that aspires to hold office, for anybody who's held office, or for anybody who has a job associated with politics, this is verboten. I am in the ground, and the dirt is being thrown on top of my coffin. But what I want to tell you is that among the public, this is absolutely overwhelming. I suggest to you that this is the biggest head-in-the-sand issue that exists in this country today. In New Mexico, I am being approached rapid fire with people saying "right on" with your statements regarding the war on drugs. And I want to suggest to you that it's a 97-to-3 difference among the public. This has been unbelievable. To give you one example, two elderly ladies came up to my table during dinner the other night, Gertrude and Mabel. They said, "We're teachers and we just think your school voucher idea sucks. But your position on the war on drugs . . . Right on! Right on!"

"Drugs and crime go together like gum and
sidewalks, and 'legalizing' the drugs won't
change that sticky connection."

Illegal Drugs Should Not Be Legalized

Ray Wisher

In the following viewpoint Ray Wisher argues that legalizing drugs would not lead to a reduction in crime. Addicts steal in order to finance their drug habit; even if drugs are legalized, he contends that addicts still will not be able to afford their habits and so will continue their lives of crime. Legalizing drugs will only destroy more lives, he concludes, and damage society. Wisher is a police detective in Florida.

As you read, consider the following questions:

1. According to Wisher, what percentage of his caseload is drug-related?
2. How many more murders are committed under the influence of drugs than are committed in order to buy drugs, as cited by the author?
3. In Wisher's view, what is the chance that a drug user will spend time in jail?

Ray Wisher, "Joint at the Hip," *American Enterprise Online*, June 2001. Copyright © 2001 by the American Enterprise Institute for Public Policy Research. Reprinted with permission of The American Enterprise, a magazine of Politics, Business, and Culture. On the web at www.TAEmag.com.

My partner, Tony G., tossed another manila crime file towards me in disgust. I picked it up and read the details. Apparently, a business owner had hired a man to do some work and the guy ended up stealing a bunch of equipment. The suspect pawned the property and used the money to buy crack. I pointed to my stack of files. "I've got a couple just like this in my pile." Typically, the wrongdoer doesn't even try to hide the fact he is stealing. When caught, he falls back on the excuse that he's an addict and needs treatment, not punishment. Yet in my experience, the vast majority of addicts either resist any treatment or fail to follow through with it.

Drugs Lead to Crime

As my fellow cops can tell you, drugs and crime go together like gum and sidewalks, and "legalizing" the drugs won't change that sticky connection. Drugs will continue to lead to crime and to drag non-drug-takers into the crime scene.

Take the property crimes that make up much of my workload. Even if drugs were legalized and (as proponents claim) drug prices fell as a result, the typical addict would still end up unable to support his habit because the typical addict can't hold a job, period. Nor can he bring himself to stay in treatment without some outside coercion.

One teenage girl mixed up with some of my worst juvenile thieves, for example, explains that her parents and the parents of her criminal friends are all generous with money, and the gang never lacked cash for the cheap drugs like marijuana. But while their indulgent moms and dads gave them enough handouts to buy all the beer and joints they could consume, there wasn't enough cash for the $100 or so a night needed for powder cocaine—"the champagne of drugs," as she puts it. And so she and her friends began stealing from relatives, neighbors, classmates, strangers. If pot, the drug most of these kids started out with, had been legal, they and many more like them would only have been encouraged to move on, as they did, to harder drugs which require crime to afford.

Nor would legal drugs have kept this girl from the many problems she experienced. Her drug-taking caused her to hang out with thug wannabes; it caused her "A" student grades to tumble; it diminished her resistance to promiscuity and hooliganism. After she joined the drug scene, her self-respect and her respect for other people and their property went out the window. The street cost of her narcotics was only a minor factor in what you could call her de-civilization.

A Threat on Many Levels

Drug abuse is a threat on many levels. For one thing, the crimes committed by druggies are a considerable drain on both our economy and police time. Recently one of my suspects, who stole equipment from his employer, was arrested for stealing and pawning property from another set of victims. He told the judge he was out of control and needed help. The judge, considering thieving non-violent, released him on a small bond. Back out on the street, the suspect continues to steal to pay for crack—a very cheap drug, by the way—while I struggle to compile the necessary paperwork to make an arrest on his *first* set of offenses.

Drugs make the addict do things he would not normally do. One of my first calls when I was assigned to take photos of crime scenes was to document a grandmother who had a claw hammer embedded in her skull by her grandson. She had refused to give him ten dollars so he could buy more crack. When crack arrived in our area scores and scores of crimes followed, ranging from bad checks and prostitution to robbery and murder, all of them related directly to crack's addictive power.

Drug Users Are Thieves

The vast majority of criminals we arrest are drug users to one degree or another. There is a saying around here, "Not all thieves are dopers but all dopers are thieves." One local "fence" supplied drugs to an entire group of high schoolers by trading them their highs in return for guns, jewelry, and other goods the kids stole.

I always ask those who argue for the legalization of drugs the simple question, "Even if you legalize it, how does the addict pay for it?" The question is usually followed by a pregnant pause and a bewildered look. Is this country prepared to pay each addict whatever his habit costs, whenever he demands it? If not, then legalizing drugs won't lower the number of bad guys I have to catch.

Example of Horrific Behavior

If you don't believe that drugs can take decent, normal people and spin them around to horrific behavior, let me give you a couple of ordinary examples. In one case I had, a woman's house was burglarized; her checkbook, jewelry, and clothes were taken. The victim believed her addicted friend was responsible; so I interviewed the suspect's husband. He told me she was indeed addicted to crack. In the beginning she took powder cocaine occasionally "for recreational use." Then she tried crack once, and the next thing he knew she had left him and two children to prostitute herself on the street.

He was trying to divorce her but couldn't find her to serve the papers as she moved from one cheap motel to another. She had taken up with drug dealers from Fort Myers and begun passing bad checks and stealing. To help me find her, he handed me a photo of the family—a smiling, clear-eyed, attractive blonde with her loving husband and two children, a boy and girl around nine or ten. As I took the picture, he dropped his eyes from mine, perhaps feeling guilty he hadn't found a way to save his wife. (This is not unusual. Crackheads are great at affixing blame to others.)

When I finally found and arrested her weeks later, she bore little resemblance to the woman in the family portrait. Gaunt, desperate, alternately lying and begging for forgiveness, she went through the classic withdrawal symptoms while I dealt with her.

Tony G. had a similar case, where the son of a retired police officer stole the old man's four pistols and sold them for crack. (Crackheads usually steal from their parents at some point.) After one of the guns was used in a shooting, I went with Tony to a small, dirty motel to interview the skinny suspect. He denied everything, even though the boxes for the pistols were found in his car trunk. He zigzagged between complete denial and trying to work a deal with us so he wouldn't go to jail (the shame of prison meant nothing to him, but the prospect of no crack was horrifying).

We arrested him a week later. It was a sad sight to see the son of a decent, law-abiding man, crammed in the little motel room with his own six-year-old son. Trash was everywhere, along with half-eaten food and dirty clothes. His son, a bright little boy, sat reading a book while we waited for his grandfather to pick him up. He didn't know what was going on, but his dad figured out Tony was trying to avoid having the kid see his father arrested. So the suspect began complaining aloud about how we were ruining his Christmas with his boy. I sat with the kid, reading stories and talking about school. The father convinced Tony he wanted one more minute with the boy. Released from Tony's grip, the guy briefly hugged his son—then lit up his last cigarette, which was what he really wanted all along.

A quick survey of my caseload reveals that about 85 percent of my current cases are drug related. The crimes range from burglary to assault to credit card fraud. One victim had her house ransacked, and within days her checks began showing up at stores throughout the county. She starting getting notices from check-clearing companies all over the country. The paperwork drove her crazy, not to mention ruining her credit.

Check forging is big business in the drug economy. Stolen blank checks are sold or traded for drugs with dealers, who then either resell them or send out their street whores to write them at stores. Many stores just swipe the check and let the purchase go through without checking ID.

A while back we had a series of purse snatchings done by a white male and his two white female crackhead prostitutes. They targeted elderly women, knocking them down then taking their purses. Before we had even finished writing up a crime report the young women would be at a grocery store or a large discount store passing their checks.

Under the Influence

In addition to the crimes committed by drug users to obtain money for drugs, sometimes drugs themselves simply cause crime. More than four times as many murders are committed *under the influence* of drugs as are committed to get money to *buy* drugs, according to federal and state data. Many needless lesser offenses are committed by people while in a drugged condition.

I have arrested countless people, mostly teens, who have broken into homes, been involved in brawls, assaulted females, stolen cars, and committed similar offenses, only to hear the excuse that "I was so stoned/blasted/high I don't remember much of what happened." Many of the people I arrest say that if they weren't on drugs they would never have done what they did. And I believe them.

An Argument for Legalization?

Drugs like heroin and cocaine are not dangerous because they are illegal, they are illegal because they are dangerous.

But still, let's grant the drug legalizers a grain of salt. Let's give them their statistics and philosophical arguments: Assume alcohol and cigarettes create addictions, ruin families, cause depression, countless traffic fatalities and increase the incidence of homicide and suicide.

How is this supposed to be an argument for legalizing another drug like them?

Steve Park, *Johns Hopkins News-Letter*, April 12, 2001.

I asked one of our lieutenants and one of our narcotics officers, "Of all the crimes you see, how many would you guess involve drugs, excluding alcohol?" The narc officer thought about 75 percent, the lieutenant, around 60. In my case, I would say about seven out of ten. One example is a heavy-duty doper I have known for years who tried to get his ex-girlfriend to have sex with another girl one drunken, drugged-up night. She refused and tried to leave. He followed her outside and hit her in the head with a two by four. He forced the other girl to grope the victim, then rammed his fist up the victim's anal cavity. He took her unconscious body and dumped it on a canal bank in a pile of ants and then tried to cover the crime by burning the victim's car. The flames from the car saved the young girl's life; the fire department responded and found her.

So when people ask if drugs cause crime, the answer is a resounding yes. A couple of months ago, a local juvenile doper robbed a drug dealer's girlfriend (she is also a drug dealer). He wanted money and drugs so he could get away from an upcoming juvenile detention stint. As a result of the robbery, the girl and three other goons came into our city and attacked an acquaintance of the robber—a young man who is a peaceful, hippie-style drug user whose biggest thrill is following a particular rock band around. He was beaten, kidnapped, and taken to another home where the four criminals kicked in the door looking for the offending juvenile doper. Eventually, they found him, and when they did they shot him in the chest twice. To tally the events, we suffered over a three-day period one robbery, two batteries, one aggravated battery, one home invasion, one kidnapping, and one attempted murder—all over drugs.

The Biggest Threat

Yet the biggest threat is not the hardened criminal drug abuser. The biggest threat today is the drugs themselves and what they do to young people. "Drugs today are so much more potent than before it's scary," notes our narcotics sergeant. Heroin, Ecstasy, marijuana, cocaine, crystal meth, pills of all descriptions—all these drugs are far more dangerous than before. Just recently a version of Ecstasy has come out with heroin added to the original chemical concoction. It won't be long before that begins to run up a death toll, given how popular Ecstasy is with high schoolers today.

Crackheads are often so hooked that when they see a cop coming they won't even run but just start puffing hard on the pipe to get every last bit they can. Crystal meth, a fairly new drug not yet common in Southwest Florida (but on the march), has the opposite effect. It hops up users so much it could force a good Rambo imitation out of Woody Allen. Meth users get so agitated they frequently chew holes through their own cheeks.

A Slide into Self-Destruction

Teens who get hooked on drugs like Xanax or Ecstasy often smoke marijuana heavily as well, and thus begin a slide into self-destruction that often takes their families and friends with them. I have seen white middle-class girls and boys as young as 12 stoned out of their minds on pot or zannies (a narcotics officer pal sees them as young as ten). I've worked case upon case where the mother and father will beg us for some kind of answer to their kid's out-of-control behavior. The sad fact is we don't have an answer.

Drugs have become such an accepted part of our society that using them has lost much of its stigma. And if you don't believe me, look at www.ecstacy.org and its glowing testimonials of father and daughter tripping together, its recommendations for how best to indulge in Ecstasy during pregnancy, and so forth. One of my biggest challenges is convincing middle-class parents that there is a problem. Usually the kid's behavior is so obvious the whole affair is a matter of parents' being unwilling to acknowledge the white elephant sitting in their living room. Sometimes parents who are normally law-abiding end up obstructing cops like me—lying to us, concealing stolen property, and worse—to protect their drug-using children.

That only makes things worse. Once they're in the drug culture, most of these kids will start to commit crimes that range from the silly to the devastating. Kids who like to get high but are afraid to steal will suddenly discover that they're helping their druggie friends transport stolen goods. They increasingly find themselves connected to lying and scams, weapons-carrying, and violence. Often teens start dealing drugs just to support their own habits. The cold hard truth is, if drugs were not tolerated, the vast majority of the crimes would never occur.

Little Chance of Jail

Despite horror stories told by the drug legalization lobby which claim "harmless casual drug users are being locked up by the thousands for trying a single joint," the unfortunate reality is that unless you are some kind of drug trafficker, the chance of spending significant time in jail for drug use today is tiny. In Florida, a state with relatively stern anti-drug laws, you're basically safe unless we catch you with 25 pounds of marijuana. And if we catch you with 24 pounds and 15 ounces, there's still a good chance you can avoid prison because of sentencing guidelines and statutes. You can walk around with dozens of Ecstasy pills in your pocket and flaunt the same feeling of safety. As a narcotics officer here says, "You'll go to jail a lot faster for fighting with your wife, or driving after three beers, or committing a crime as a cop, than you will for dealing or shooting up drugs."

Nationwide, seven out of ten drug offenders who have no prior record avoid any prison sentence. This includes major traffickers. If you look only at those arrested for drug possession, figures from the U.S. Bureau of Justice Statistics show that the vast majority avoid prison *even if they have previous convictions.*

Unless and until our society becomes much more hard-nosed against drugs—a possibility which seems remote, especially when the generation now in power are veterans of the anything-goes 1960s—there will continue to be hordes of damaged human beings passing through our homes, workplaces, communities, and courtrooms.

"As the sophistication of pharmaceuticals develops exponentially each year, the lines we draw between legal and illegal . . . will become more and more arbitrary."

The Distinction Between Legal and Illegal Drugs Is Arbitrary

Andrew Sullivan

Andrew Sullivan points out in the following viewpoint that the war on drugs is not a war on all drugs but only on some drugs. He questions why some drugs are illegal when others, which have similar properties and produce similar effects, are entirely legal. He maintains that there is no sense in the laws that make one drug legal and a similar drug illegal. He contends that as drug-making technologies continue to produce ever more sophisticated drugs, the distinction between all kinds of drugs, from caffeine to Ecstacy, will become even more blurred. Sullivan is a senior editor at the *New Republic* magazine.

As you read, consider the following questions:

1. How are Ecstasy and Prozac similar, according to Sullivan?
2. To what substances does Sullivan compare methamphetamine?
3. Which medicinal drugs also have high recreational street value, in Sullivan's opinion?

The most frustrating part of the interminable debate about the "war on drugs" is the word "drugs." Strictly speaking, after all, there is no war on drugs in this country; there is a war on some drugs. America boasts a vast legitimate pharmaceutical industry, and personal expenditures on its products go up every year. Very, very few of us go even a week without taking some kind of drug, be it an over-the-counter cold medicine, a doctor-prescribed medication, or a self-medicated legal substance—a cigarette, a shot of tequila, a double espresso, a McFlurry. And the variety and sophistication of these substances are growing as fast as their use. Do you remember the day when you could simply ask for a cup of coffee and no further elaboration was required?

The salient question behind the "drug" war, then, is not simply the usual libertarian-authoritarian conundrum. It's much simpler: What is the criterion that makes one drug the object of a "war" in which millions are incarcerated for illegal use and another drug the object of a vast marketing machine through which millions are regularly sold to and hooked?

A Question with an Elusive Answer

The more you think about the question, the more elusive the answer becomes. Once upon a time, medicine was relatively unsophisticated. The few medicinal drugs there were saved lives or cured obvious debilitating illnesses; the few recreational drugs there were gave people pleasure or excitement or oblivion and were regulated on an ad hoc but vaguely sane basis. In a puritanical culture, drugs that were extremely pleasurable, physically harmful, and highly addictive—opium, cocaine, heroin—were banned. Drugs that were mildly pleasurable, slightly unhealthy, and less addictive—caffeine, nicotine, alcohol—were milked for profit and tax revenues. Few pretended this scheme was entirely coherent—permitting addictive, destructive booze while banning nonaddictive, benign pot made no real sense—but it seemed a practical balance between the right to personal pleasure and the need for social calm. The one attempt to be coherent, Prohibition, proved the dangers of consistent logic in social policy.

And then technology had its way. It seems to me that the last decade or so has largely invalidated whatever sanity lay behind this practicable scheme. Our deeper understanding of the chemical effect of even a candy bar has made us think about everything we consume in pharmacological terms. (You can partly thank the Food and Drug Administration's labeling for that.) And our ability to take pharmaceutical substances and alter them in minuscule ways has further blurred the distinction between "good" and "bad" chemicals. The result is a hopelessly contradictory scheme in which fat-drenched hamburgers—partly responsible for heart disease, our leading cause of death—are celebrated, while marijuana, consumed with little harm by millions, is stigmatized to the point of incarceration.

Differences in Degree

And these are the easy cases. Further up the chemical-sophistication ladder, the ironies only multiply. Take the designer drug Ecstasy. "E" is now classed in the same group of illegal drugs as heroin. But as recently as the 1980s it was completely legal; Merck patented it in 1914. E works by flooding the brain for a few hours with serotonin, the "happy" chemical, a substance our body naturally produces but in much smaller and more consistent amounts. Now compare Prozac. Prozac and its sister and successor drugs help regulate the production of serotonin for people with suppressed or unstable serotonin levels. The effect of such drugs is far less intense than that of Ecstasy—and the method by which serotonin is released and moderated is far subtler. But the substance being manipulated is the same. Indeed, people who regularly take Prozac tend to find that E barely affects their mood at all. Their serotonin problem is already fixed.

Yes, there are differences in degree here, and some in kind. Long-term, persistent use of Ecstasy has been correlated with depression. But long-term use of Prozac may affect the structural composition of the brain as well. Neither is clearly dangerous unless taken in massive doses. Both are designed to make people "happier." What rationale is there in making one drug illegal and marketing the other to literally millions every year?

Similarly, Starbucks profits by marketing coffee, a legal

163

Kelley. © 2003 by Steve Kelley. Reprinted with permission.

substance that addictively wires people for hours on end. Health-food stores sell stronger versions of speed in the form of pills and even chocolate. There are no laws preventing anyone from drinking ten double espressos or downing several packets of No-Doz. But one sniff of a much more concentrated methamphetamine—which might actually be less damaging to your body—can land you in jail. Similarly, you can get a dose of Xanax from your doctor and feel extremely mellow within half an hour; or you can take two puffs of pot and be a felon. Likewise, you can buy a drug from a vitamin store—androstenedione—to boost your own production of testosterone, or you can get a packet of testosterone gel on the black market (as thousands of teenage jocks do) and risk a criminal record. A growing number of "medicinal" drugs also have high "recreational" street value: painkillers like Vicodin, downers like Valium, uppers like Ritalin, and anesthetics like Ketamine.

My point is not that there is no sense at all in these distinctions. Clearly, crystal meth is more potent, more addictive, and easier to take than ten triple espressos. Clearly, excessive steroid use can wreck people's livers in ways that even massive use of legal androstenedione won't. But we're dealing here with degree as much as kind. And as the sophistication of pharmaceuticals develops exponentially each year, the lines we draw between legal and illegal, between stigmatized and accepted, will become more and more arbitrary.

Is There a Moral Difference?

In exactly the same way, the very definition of "health" is up for grabs. Do most people take Prozac for their mental health or their sense of well-being? Is there a moral difference between taking Xanax to get some sleep and smoking a joint? If someone wants to take modest amounts of anabolic steroids to look good and feel sexy, why should that be illegal when a legal, multibillion-dollar industry is aimed at achieving the same effects with the stone-age technology of swallowing creatine, eating steak, and pushing pieces of iron up and down? Similarly, human growth hormone was developed to accelerate the growth of stunted children. It's now popular among retiring baby-boomers who enjoy its rejuvenating effects on their bodies and minds. But the boomers often have to fake weight loss and impotence to get it legally. Why shouldn't retirees have access to it—not because they have an actual physical ailment but because they want to enjoy to the fullest what's left of their lives? Isn't aging the ultimate physical ailment?

I wish I knew the answer to these questions; to me they seem the ones we need to confront. The war on soft drugs is built on such logical sand that it cannot be sustained forever—just as the once-clear distinction between health and pleasure is now disintegrating, and only our residual cultural puritanism is propping it up. In a country dedicated to the pursuit of happiness, where happiness is reducible to a chemical, surely the "war on drugs" will not be the only casualty of this development.

"By tolerating [heroin] usage, we would find it easier to minimise harm."

Heroin Should Be Legalized

Bruce Anderson

In the following viewpoint Bruce Anderson asserts that when it was legal to prescribe heroin in Britain, there were few heroin addicts; they received their heroin supply from their doctors and did not have to resort to crime to finance their addictions. When Britain submitted to pressure to make heroin illegal, heroin addicts were forced to get their drug from other sources, and thus began the black market for heroin and the attendant crime. Anderson argues that heroin should once again be legalized. Illegal heroin has no guarantee of quality and can seriously damage or even kill the addict. Heroin is also the major cause of drug-related crime; if heroin is legal, crime rates will fall, Anderson contends. Anderson is the former editor at large and political editor for the *Spectator*, a British weekly magazine.

As you read, consider the following questions:
1. Why is methadone a poor substitute for heroin, according to the author?
2. According to Anderson, how much does the average heroin addict steal per year?
3. What is one of the complications of legalizing drugs, in Anderson's opinion?

Bruce Anderson, "Dead Children Are Not Reliable Counsellors: It Is Time to Legalise Heroin," *Spectator*, vol. 288, March 9, 2002, p. 10. Copyright © 2002 by The Spectator Ltd. Reproduced by permission.

They were heart-rending photographs. A young girl, whose sweet face sang of the hope and joy of youth; a couple of years later, she is a broken, beggarly creature, who perishes in squalor and despair. What is this hideous strength which can transform good into evil? Surely we must deploy all the power of the law to curb its malignancy.

If only the drug question were that simple. But emotion and dead children are not reliable counsellors. If prohibition could have solved the problem, Rachel Whitear would still be alive. Her death was further evidence that our present policy has failed and is doomed to unending failure; that however well-intentioned its authors may be, they are adding to the sum of human misery.

Heroin

Let us take the hardest case: heroin. A generation ago, there was no heroin problem in Britain. A few doctors, most of whom were themselves junkies, kept a few thousand addicts supplied with heroin, on prescription. In those days, there was, if anything, a negative correlation between heroin addiction and crime.

Then the Americans agitated for a tough UN [United Nations] Convention on heroin. Like most proposals to erode our national sovereignty, this appeared to emanate from high-mindedness; it is not easy to generate the political courage to dissent from a widely supported proposal to tackle drug abuse. So the United Kingdom agreed, thus creating a heroin problem and a crime problem.

It became almost impossible for doctors to prescribe heroin. Instead, the addicts were offered methadone, which is almost as dangerous, but much less pleasurable. In response, the junkies went elsewhere.

Demand Created an Industry

Their consumer demand then created an industry, whose annual turnover is now estimated to be almost £5 billion. There are some 270,000 addicts, and most of them resort to theft to pay for their drugs. The best estimate is that the average addict steals about £13,000 a year, but that understates the problem. If an addict is stealing goods rather than cash, it needs an awful lot of mobile phones to raise £13,000.

In response to all this, the law has not been silent. The criminal justice system is eloquent with heroin-related pains and penalties: up to seven years in prison for possession, a possible life sentence for supply. But it is not working. The rewards for trafficking are so great; the craving of the addicted is so intense. The cash and the customers pour into the black market, giving dealers and addicts, some of whom raise money by recruiting new customers, every incentive to prey upon the vulnerable young, like Rachel Whitear.

There are two further issues, one practical, the other philosophical. A heroin addict who has the equivalent of a lucky liver can live an almost normal life for an almost average lifespan, as long as he only indulges in good-quality heroin. But if the trade is illicit, there is no guarantee of quality. Addicts who sell to other addicts are especially likely to deal in adulterated heroin, and those who inject themselves with adulterated heroin are playing Russian roulette with their blood supply. That may have helped to kill Miss Whitear.

Bigger Problems than Drug Abuse

But there is a more fundamental objection to the present arrangements. They are based on no coherent theory of the state. The anti-libertarians have a clear and respectable case; it is possible to argue that the state should regulate the private behaviour of adults. If so, however, why stop—or start—with the currently illegal drugs? Nicotine addiction is responsible for more deaths than all other drugs combined and multiplied; broken families create far more human misery; abortion is a much greater moral evil. If all mood-altering substances were legal, alcohol might well give rise to the greatest number of social problems. So a practical and consistent authoritarian ought to regard bans on abortion, adultery, cigarettes, divorce and drinking as greater priorities than prohibiting heroin or cocaine.

The counter-argument maintains that the private behaviour of adults is none of the state's business. This is acknowledged in many other areas, so why not in hard drugs? It is the only position consistent with the rest of the workings of the modern state. Perhaps drug-users should launch a class action against the government, in that its behaviour has violated the implicit separation of powers between the modern state and its citizens—while the victims of drug-related crime press another lawsuit, to demand compensation for their sufferings, which have arisen from the state's failure to observe the contemporary social contract.

Legalisation

I have concentrated on heroin, because it is the major cause of drug-related crime. Few people rob to sustain a cocaine habit, and the principal difficulty about legalising cocaine is the ease with which it can be turned into crack. Given that crack induces psychopathic/psychotic behaviour, even an ardent libertarian should have no difficulty in arguing for a continued ban; legalising crack would be the equivalent of allowing drunks to drive at 80mph in a built-up area. But if heroin and cocaine were legalised for adults, it would be easier for the police to concentrate their fire on crack—and on other criminal acts. . . . The Lord Chief Justice implored the judiciary to take account of the bursting prisons before passing gaol sentences. If heroin were legalised, Harry Woolf [British author of several books on criminal justice] would have no need to worry: the prisons would be full of empty cells.

As for marijuana, the law is already spliffed. Decriminalisation is now virtually universal. Yet it is the most foolish of all solutions. It leaves the market in the hands of the criminals, some of whom use their increasingly easy takings to move into the much more lucrative heroin market. There is only one solution to the marijuana conundrum: to tax it as heavily as is possible without encouraging a black market, and then allow it to be sold to those over 18, while banning advertising—and with swingeing fines for any sale to under 18s (the same rules ought to apply to tobacco).

In an ideal society, drugs would be freely available, and no one would take them. In the actual world, legalisation is complicated and dangerous. The first complication is age. Given that the young are now allowed to buy cigarettes or be sodomised at the age of 16 while they can vote or die for their country at 18, which also used to be the age at which the death sentence applied, it must be illogical to place a higher age limit than 18 for the purchase of heroin or cocaine. Yet we know how young in judgment the average 18-year-old can be. So those of us who advocate legalisation have to take one argument on the chin. The legalisation of hard drugs would encourage experiments by some youngsters who are currently deterred by illegality. Through folly or metabolism, a quota of those youngsters would move on to addiction. Some would be destroyed.

That price would have to be paid: it is worth paying. It might seem [cold-blooded], but there is a trade-off between harm and usage. At the moment we are trying to suppress both, and failing to deal with either. By tolerating usage, we would find it easier to minimise harm.

"[The drug law] is the one thing that stands between their children and the pusher. Take away the sanction of the law and they know . . . that the drugs problem will get worse."

Legalizing Heroin Will Harm the Poor

Katie Grant

Katie Grant is a columnist and book reviewer for the *Spectator*, a weekly British magazine. In the following viewpoint she argues that drug legalization is a class issue. If heroin were legalized, the middle class would be able to afford to buy their drugs from an approved government source but the poor would still be forced to buy heroin from black market pushers. Grant also asserts that it is the illegality of heroin that keeps many children from trying the drug in the first place. Drug addiction is a serious problem, she maintains, one that will not be fixed by legalizing drugs.

As you read, consider the following questions:
1. How do socially deprived communities see the current debate about drug legalization, according to Grant?
2. What leads to drug-taking in poor communities, in the author's opinion?
3. By what age have nearly all children in Scotland been offered drugs, as cited by Grant?

Katie Grant, "A Fix for the Middle Classes," *Spectator*, vol. 288, March 16, 2002, p. 20. Copyright © 2002 by The Spectator Ltd. Reproduced by permission.

Bruce Anderson called . . . for the legalisation of drugs, and his remarks were timely. In Scotland, Dr Richard Simpson, the Holyrood Parliament's deputy justice minister, has echoed Mr Anderson's sentiments, if not his solution, by drawing an official line under Scotland's 30-year war on drugs. 'The only time you will hear me use terms such as "War On Drugs" or "Just Say No" is to denigrate them,' he said. When Bruce Anderson, a glowering bull mastiff on a short fuse, and Richard Simpson, a gentle bearded collie with herding instincts, find common ground, something is clearly up. What is up, of course, is that both men have been upset by the images of the black and bloated body of a pretty girl killed by a bad heroin fix.

A Class Issue

Doubtless both Mr Anderson and Dr Simpson—and the Lib-Dems, who have just called for the legalisation of cannabis—will be congratulated by professionals who are fond of a decent spliff, toss down the odd E and have no wish to see their experimenting children turned into criminals. But their contributions, while worthy, ignore the great big difficulty that lies at the very heart of the drugs debate. Drugs are a class issue. If everyone were as clever and well-to-do as Mr Anderson, or as educated and thoughtful as Dr Simpson, we could legalise drugs tomorrow. Everybody would have an equal opportunity to take them or to resist them. The libertarian argument that forms the core of the legalisers' camp—that the state has no place in regulating the private behaviour of individuals—would be unanswerable.

Yet while flawless logic and consistency of approach—the academically unimpeachable grounds on which Mr Anderson stands—are splendidly appealing to those sneaking a post-glass-of-claret snooze behind copies of the *Times* in the Reform Club, they look quite different if you are sitting on a grimy copy of the *Daily Record* eating a poke of soggy chips in a bleak, rubbish-strewn stairwell on one of Glasgow's desolate peripheral estates. A mother watching her newly literate four-year-old spelling out 'fuck the Pope' or 'Lesley's a f—c—' from the graffiti which, along with used syringes and the odd condom, decorate the slide in the derelict park, will not be persuaded by Mr Anderson's solution to the drugs problem.

To many of the parents on Scotland's sink estates, the fact that the law does not work is irrelevant. To them, it is the one thing that stands between their children and the pusher. Take away the sanction of the law and they know, with almost religious certainty, that the drugs problem will get worse. To these women, legalisation is the path to hell, and they are already halfway there. They may well be open to debates about how the petty criminality that funds a drug habit should be dealt with, but they see debates about legalisation as being the middle classes at play.

Groups such as Mothers Against Drugs laugh when you say that at least the supply of heroin will be controlled if it is legalised. Controlled for whom, they ask? For the middle classes, perhaps, who would go to official outlets to get their fix. But the plight of the socially excluded, the underclasses, those whose chaotic lives suit street dealers perfectly, would be no better off. Drug barons, unwilling to give up without a fight, would simply undercut the official outlets using the existing networks. A £1 coin may not be much to a doctor's daughter, but it is a lot to a 22-year-old on benefit. If using cheaper heroin meant taking a bit of a risk, they would think the risk worth taking, just as they go to a loan shark instead of to the bank.

How the Drug War Is Seen

This is how, in socially deprived communities, the current debates about drugs are seen: as the middle classes taking care of their own. So long as middle-class youngsters can take heroin, cocaine or Ecstasy safely (E-safety kits are very much in vogue at the moment), then the drugs problem will be deemed to have been solved. If the risks to their children posed by impure heroin are removed, Tory grandees and New Labour groupies will be satisfied—particularly since, if the children of the well-to-do fall into addiction, they can always be sent by their parents into private rehab centres. Addicts from the underclasses will, of course, not be so lucky. Places on state-funded rehab or detox courses are few and far between.

Of course there is an argument that legalising drugs would

cut crime. But is this not just a fudge that allows politicians and society, on the back of blissfully decreasing crime statistics, to ignore with clear consciences the underlying causes that lead to drug-taking on sink estates: lives bereft, generation after generation, of any meaning or structure, appalling living conditions, dismal, third-rate education, poverty of aspiration, moral turpitude and welfare dependency?

Estimated Numbers (in Thousands) of Lifetime Users of Heroin, by Age Group: 2000 and 2001

| | | | AGE GROUP (Years) | | | | | |
| | Total | | 2–17 | | 18–25 | | 26 or Older | |
	2000	2001	2000	2001	2000	2001	2000	2001
Heroin	2,779	3,091	84	76	403	474	2,292	2,541
Smoke Heroin	990	1,219	33	31	156	181	801	1,007
Sniff or Snort Heroin	1,817	2,014	30	36	236	296	1,551	1,682

SAMHSA, Office of Applied Studies, National Household Survey on Drug Abuse, 2000 and 2001.

But perhaps this is the point. Who really cares if coarse, foul-mouthed, feckless single parent Karen McNumpty and her hideous boyfriend die in the gutter of a long-term heroin addiction funded by pimping and prostitution? If legalisation does not help them, so what? The unspoken thought seems to be that the important thing is to help others who are more deserving; others, indeed, such as Rachel Whitear, a middle-class girl whose 'sweet face sang of the hope and joy of youth', to quote Mr Anderson. She has elicited his sympathy in a way that Karen McNumpty—graceless at 12, pregnant at 16, an addict by 19—never could. Mr Anderson thinks that legalisation might help girls like Rachel—and indeed it might. But where does that leave Karen? Should a civilised society enact legislation that is really designed to help only one of its constituent parts?

A New Strategy Is Needed

By the age of 15, nearly all children in Scotland have been offered drugs. Some will swell the ranks of the 56,000 addicts already registered. Of the 2.6 million offences committed each year in Glasgow alone, 90 per cent, according to police, are drug-related. One child in every 100 takes drugs before their 11th birthday. Clearly, a new strategy is needed.

But let us never forget that there are two worlds out there, one that operates through logic and consistency and another in which things are much more chaotic and complicated. Those pushing for the legalisation of hard drugs must not let their view of how things should be prevent them from seeing how things are. All middle-class parents want reassurance that, should their children take heroin, they will not die. All middle-class taxpayers want the crime statistics, and therefore their insurance premiums, to fall. But although our world is run by the middle classes, it is those whose lot in life is rather less comfortable who would bear the real brunt of moves towards the legalisation of hard drugs. They do not seem to be full of enthusiasm for the idea. As one addict, now on his second methadone programme, told me . . . and I paraphrase for ease of comprehension, 'Legalisation? What a joke. Christ! What planet are they living on? God, those bloody chatterers. They'll be the death of us all.'

"It makes little sense to send people to jail for using a drug that, in terms of its harmfulness, should be categorized somewhere between alcohol and tobacco on one hand and caffeine on the other."

Marijuana Should Be Legalized

Rich Lowry

Marijuana is a relatively harmless drug, argues Rich Lowry in the following viewpoint. In fact, he asserts, alcohol and tobacco are responsible for the deaths of hundreds of thousands of Americans every year while marijuana has never killed anyone. In addition, most marijuana users slow down or stop smoking the drug as they enter their thirties, he claims. Lowry maintains that the prohibition against marijuana is based more on cultural prejudice than on facts and should be repealed. Lowry is the editor of the *National Review*, a conservative weekly magazine.

As you read, consider the following questions:
1. What does California's Proposition 36 require for first- and second-time nonviolent drug offenders, according to Lowry?
2. According to the report by the Institute of Medicine cited by the author, how many Americans have tried marijuana or hashish at least once?
3. According to the IOM report cited by Lowry, what percentage of men who used marijuana daily had never used any other drug?

Rarely do trial balloons burst so quickly. During the [2001] British campaign, Tory shadow home secretary Ann Widdecombe had no sooner proposed tougher penalties for marijuana possession than a third of her fellow Tory shadow-cabinet ministers admitted to past marijuana use. Widdecombe immediately had to back off. The controversy reflected a split in the party, with the confessors attempting to embarrass Widdecombe politically. But something deeper was at work as well: a nascent attempt to reckon honestly with a drug that has been widely used by baby boomers and their generational successors, a tentative step toward a squaring by the political class of its personal experience with the drastic government rhetoric and policies regarding marijuana.

The American debate hasn't yet reached such a juncture, even though [the 2000] presidential campaign featured one candidate [George W. Bush] who pointedly refused to answer questions about his past drug use and another who—according to [Al] Gore biographer Bill Turque—spent much of his young adulthood smoking dope and skipping through fields of clover (and still managed to become one of the most notoriously uptight and ambitious politicians in the country). In recent years, the debate over marijuana policy has centered on the question of whether the drug should be available for medicinal purposes. . . . Drug warriors call medical marijuana the camel's nose under the tent for legalization, and so—for many of its advocates— it is. Both sides in the medical-marijuana controversy have ulterior motives, which suggests it may be time to stop debating the nose and move on to the full camel.

An Increase in Liberalization Measures

Already, there has been some action. About a dozen states have passed medical-marijuana laws in recent years, and California voters approved Proposition 36, mandating treatment instead of criminal penalties for all first- and second-time nonviolent drug offenders. Proponents of the initiative plan to export it to Ohio, Michigan, and Florida. Most such liberalization measures fare well at the polls—California's passed with 61 percent of the vote—as long as they aren't perceived as going too far. Loosen, but don't legalize, seems to be the general public attitude, even as almost every politician still fears departing from Bill Bennett orthodoxy on the issue. But listen carefully to the drug warriors, and you can hear some of them quietly reading marijuana out of the drug war. James Q. Wilson, for instance, perhaps the nation's most convincing advocate for drug prohibition, is careful to set marijuana aside from his arguments about the potentially ruinous effects of legalizing drugs.

There is good reason for this, since it makes little sense to send people to jail for using a drug that, in terms of its harmfulness, should be categorized somewhere between alcohol and tobacco on one hand and caffeine on the other. According to common estimates, alcohol and tobacco kill hundreds of thousands of people a year. In contrast, there is as a practical matter no such thing as a lethal overdose of marijuana. Yet federal law makes possessing a single joint punishable by up to a year in prison, and many states have similar penalties. There are about 700,000 marijuana arrests in the United States every year, roughly 80 percent for possession. Drug warriors have a strange relationship with these laws: They dispute the idea that anyone ever actually goes to prison for mere possession, but at the same time resist any suggestion that laws providing for exactly that should be struck from the books. So, in the end, one of the drug warriors' strongest arguments is that the laws they favor aren't enforced—we're all liberalizers now.

Gateway to Nowhere

There has, of course, been a barrage of government-sponsored anti-marijuana propaganda over the last two decades, but the essential facts are clear: Marijuana is widely used, and for the vast majority of its users is nearly harmless and represents a temporary experiment or enthusiasm. A 1999 report by the Institute of Medicine—a highly credible outfit that is part of the National Academy of Sciences— found that "in 1996, 68.6 million people—32% of the U.S. population over 12 years old—had tried marijuana or hashish at least once in their lifetime, but only 5% were current users." The academic literature talks of "maturing out" of marijuana use the same way college kids grow out of backpacks and [philosopher Frederick] Nietzsche. Most marijuana users are between the ages of 18 and 25, and use plummets after age 34, by which time children and mortgages have blunted the appeal of rolling paper and bongs. Authors Robert J. MacCoun and Peter Reuter—drug-war skeptics, but cautious ones— point out in their new book *Drug War Heresies* that "among 26 to 34 year olds who had used the drug daily sometime in their life in 1994, only 22 percent reported that they had used it in the past year."

Marijuana prohibitionists have for a long time had trouble maintaining that marijuana itself is dangerous, so they instead have relied on a bank shot—marijuana's danger is that it leads to the use of drugs that are actually dangerous. This is a way to shovel all the effects of heroin and cocaine onto marijuana. . . . It is called the "gateway theory," and has been so thoroughly discredited that it is still dusted off only by the most tendentious of drug warriors. The theory's difficulty begins with a simple fact: Most people who use marijuana, even those who use it with moderate frequency, don't go on to use any other illegal drug. According to the Institute of Medicine report, "Of 34 to 35 year old men who had used marijuana 10–99 times by the age 24–25, 75% never used any other illicit drug." As Lynn Zimmer and John Morgan point out in their exhaustive book *Marijuana Myths/Marijuana Facts* the rates of use of hard drugs have more to do with their fashionability than their connection to marijuana. In 1986, near the peak of the cocaine epidemic, 33 percent of high-school seniors who had used marijuana also had tried cocaine, but by 1994 only 14 percent of marijuana users had gone on to use cocaine.

Faulty Reasoning

Then, there is the basic faulty reasoning behind the gateway theory. Since marijuana is the most widely available and least dangerous illegal drug, it makes sense that people inclined to use other harder-to-find drugs will start with it first—but this tells us little or nothing about marijuana itself or about most of its users. It confuses temporality with causality. Because a cocaine addict used marijuana first doesn't mean he is on cocaine *because* he smoked marijuana (again, as a factual matter this hypothetical is extremely rare—about one in 100 marijuana users becomes a regular user of cocaine). Drug warriors recently have tried to argue that research showing that marijuana acts on the brain in a way vaguely similar to cocaine and heroin—plugging into the same receptors—proves that it somehow "primes" the brain for harder drugs. But alcohol has roughly the same action, and no one argues that Budweiser creates heroin addicts. "There is no evidence," says the Institute of Medicine study, "that marijuana serves as a stepping stone on the basis of its particular physiological effect."

'You know, they warned me that smoking marijuana would lead to harder drugs.'

Bennett. © 1997 by North American Syndicate. Reprinted with permission of Clay Bennett.

The relationship between drugs and troubled teens appears to be the opposite of that posited by drug warriors—the trouble comes first, then the drugs (or, in other words, it's the kid, not the substance, who is the problem). The Institute of Medicine reports that "it is more likely that conduct disorders generally lead to substance abuse than the reverse." The British medical journal *Lancet*—in a long, careful consideration of the marijuana literature—explains that heavy marijuana use is associated with leaving high school and having trouble getting a job, but that this association wanes "when statistical adjustments are made for the fact that, compared with their peers, heavy cannabis users have poor high-school performance before using cannabis." (And, remember, this is heavy use: "adolescents who casually experiment with cannabis," according to MacCoun and Reuter, "appear to function quite well with respect to schooling and mental health.") In the same way problem kids are attracted to illegal drugs, they are drawn to alcohol and tobacco. One study found that teenage boys who smoke cigarettes daily are about ten times likelier to be diagnosed with a psychiatric disorder than non-smoking teenage boys. By the drug warrior's logic, this means that tobacco causes mental illness.

Treatment

Another arrow in the drug warriors' quiver is the number of people being treated for marijuana: If the drug is so innocuous, why do they seek, or need, treatment? Drug warriors cite figures that say that roughly 100,000 people enter drug-treatment programs every year primarily for marijuana use. But often, the punishment for getting busted for marijuana possession is treatment. According to one government study, in 1998 54 percent of people in state-run treatment programs for marijuana were sent there by the criminal-justice system. So, there is a circularity here: The drug war mandates marijuana treatment, then its advocates point to the fact of that treatment to justify the drug war. Also, people who test positive in employment urine tests often have to get treatment to keep their jobs, and panicked parents will often deliver their marijuana-smoking sons and daughters to treatment programs. This is not to deny that there is such a thing as marijuana dependence. According to *The Lancet*, "About one in ten of those who ever use cannabis become dependent on it at some time during their 4 or 5 years of heaviest use."

But it is important to realize that dependence on marijuana—apparently a relatively mild psychological phenomenon—is entirely different from dependence on cocaine and heroin. Marijuana isn't particularly addictive. One key indicator of the addictiveness of other drugs is that lab rats will self-administer them. Rats simply won't self-administer

THC, the active ingredient in marijuana. Two researchers in 1991 studied the addictiveness of caffeine, nicotine, alcohol, heroin, cocaine, and marijuana. Both ranked caffeine and marijuana as the least addictive. One gave the two drugs identical scores and another ranked marijuana as slightly less addicting than caffeine. A 1991 U.S. Department of Health and Human Services report to Congress states: "Given the large population of marijuana users and the infrequent reports of medical problems from stopping use, tolerance and dependence are not major issues at present." Indeed, no one is quite sure what marijuana treatment exactly is. As Mac-Coun and Reuter write, "Severity of addiction is modest enough that there is scarcely any research on treatment of marijuana dependence."

Marijuana as a "Gateway" Drug

Patterns in progression of drug use from adolescence to adulthood are strikingly regular. Because it is the most widely used illicit drug, marijuana is predictably the first illicit drug most people encounter. Not surprisingly, most users of other illicit drugs have used marijuana first. In fact, most drug users begin with alcohol and nicotine before marijuana—usually before they are of legal age.

In the sense that marijuana use typically precedes rather than follows initiation of other illicit drug use, it is indeed a "gateway" drug. But because underage smoking and alcohol use typically precede marijuana use, marijuana is not the most common, and is rarely the first, "gateway" to illicit drug use. There is no conclusive evidence that the drug effects of marijuana are causally linked to the subsequent abuse of other illicit drugs.

Janet E. Joy, Stanley J. Watson Jr., and John A. Benson Jr., eds., *Marijuana and Medicine: Assessing the Science Base*. Washington, DC: National Academy Press, 1999.

None of this is to say that marijuana is totally harmless. There is at least a little truth to the stereotype of the Cheech & Chong "stoner." Long-term heavy marijuana use doesn't, in the words of *The Lancet*, "produce the severe or grossly debilitating impairment of memory, attention, and cognitive function that is found with chronic heavy alcohol use," but it can impair cognitive functioning nonetheless: "These impairments are subtle, so it remains unclear how important they are for everyday functioning, and whether they are reversed after an extended period of abstinence." This, then, is the bottom-line harm of marijuana to its users: A small minority of people who smoke it may—by choice, as much as any addictive compulsion—eventually smoke enough of it for a long enough period of time to suffer impairments so subtle that they may not affect everyday functioning or be permanent. Arresting, let alone jailing, people for using such a drug seems outrageously disproportionate, which is why drug warriors are always so eager to deny that anyone ever goes to prison for it.

Fighting the Draconian Doctrine

In this contention, the drug warriors are largely right. The fact is that the current regime is really only a half-step away from decriminalization. And despite all the heated rhetoric of the drug war, on marijuana there is a quasi-consensus: Legalizers think that marijuana laws shouldn't be on the books; prohibitionists think, in effect, that they shouldn't be enforced. A reasonable compromise would be a version of the Dutch model of decriminalization, removing criminal penalties for personal use of marijuana, but keeping the prohibition on street-trafficking and mass cultivation. Under such a scenario, laws for tobacco—an unhealthy drug that is quite addictive—and for marijuana would be heading toward a sort of middle ground, a regulatory regime that controls and discourages use but doesn't enlist law enforcement in that cause. MacCoun and Reuter have concluded from the experience of decriminalizing the possession of small amounts of marijuana in the Netherlands, twelve American states in the 1970s, and parts of Australia that "the available evidence suggests that simply removing the prohibition against possession does not increase cannabis use."

Drug warriors, of course, will have none of it. They support a . . . doctrine under which no drug-war excess can ever be turned back—once a harsh law is on the books for marijuana possession, there it must remain lest the wrong "signal" be sent. "Drug use," as Bill Bennett has said, "is dangerous and immoral." But for the overwhelming majority of its users marijuana is not the least bit dangerous. (Marijuana's chief potential danger to others—its users driving while high—should, needless to say, continue to be treated as harshly as drunk driving.) As for the immorality of marijuana's use, it generally is immoral to break the law. But this is just another drug-war circularity: The marijuana laws create the occasion for this particular immorality. If it is on the basis of its effect—namely, intoxication—that Bennett considers marijuana immoral, then he has to explain why it's different from drunkenness, and why this particular sense of well-being should be banned in an America that is now the great mood-altering nation, with millions of people on Prozac and other drugs meant primarily to make them feel good.

In the end, marijuana prohibition basically relies on cultural prejudice. This is no small thing. Cultural prejudices are important. Alcohol and tobacco are woven into the very fabric of America. Marijuana doesn't have the equivalent of, say, the "brewer-patriot" Samuel Adams (its enthusiasts try to enlist George Washington, but he *grew* hemp instead of smoking it). Marijuana is an Eastern drug, and importantly for conservatives, many of its advocates over the years have looked and thought like [Beat poet] Allen Ginsberg. But that isn't much of an argument for keeping it illegal, and if marijuana started out culturally alien, it certainly isn't anymore. No wonder drug warriors have to strain for medical and scientific reasons to justify its prohibition. But once all the misrepresentations and exaggerations are stripped away, the main pharmacological effect of marijuana is that it gets people high. Or as *The Lancet* puts it, "When used in a social setting, it may produce infectious laughter and talkativeness."

"[They] may be right to claim that marijuana does not lead to physical harm. But it does produce a pathology of the soul."

Legalizing Marijuana Would Harm Society

Part I: Damon Linker; Part II: Don Feder

In Part I of the following two-part viewpoint, Damon Linker argues against legalizing marijuana. He contends that legalizing marijuana would make it widely available, thus leading to rampant drug use among youth. Moreover, the pleasure derived from smoking marijuana is a hollow pleasure that leaves a feeling of emptiness in the user's soul, he maintains. In Part II, Don Feder asserts that marijuana is responsible for turning studious, well-behaved students into teens in trouble. He claims that a study has found a direct link between marijuana use and "delinquent/depressive behavior." Linker is the associate editor of the monthly journal *First Things;* Feder is a syndicated columnist.

As you read, consider the following questions:

1. According to Linker, why is marijuana at least as lethal as tobacco?
2. How does the pleasure of smoking marijuana differ from the pleasures of mild drunkenness, in Linker's opinion?
3. According to the *Wall Street Journal* editorial cited by Feder, what happened when the Dutch legalized marijuana?

Part I: Damon Linker, "Going to Pot?" *First Things*, November 2001, p. 6. Copyright © 2001 by the Institute on Religion and Public Life. Reproduced by permission. Part II: Don Feder, "Conservative Magazine Goes to Pot," www.townhall.com, August 22, 2001. Copyright © 2001 by Creators Syndicate. Reproduced by permission.

I

It is safe to say that at some point in the not-too-distant future, America will confront the question of whether or not to legalize the use and cultivation of marijuana. A recent poll shows that support for legalization has reached its highest level since the question was first asked thirty years ago, with 34 percent supporting a liberalization of policy. Among political elites there is a growing consensus that the harsh penalties imposed on those who grow, use, and sell marijuana are disproportionate to its harmful effects. Even among conservatives, opinion seems to be shifting. Whether the change should be welcomed is another matter.

In an essay for *National Review*, Richard Lowry raises the question of whether marijuana is truly harmful—and he concludes that it isn't, or at least that it is significantly less so than any number of other drugs that are currently legal. Marijuana, he argues, "should be categorized somewhere between alcohol and tobacco on the one hand, and caffeine on the other." As evidence, he first points out that whereas "alcohol and tobacco kill hundreds of thousands of people a year," there is "no such thing as a lethal overdose of marijuana."

While this is certainly true, it is also the case that, strictly speaking, there is no such thing as a "lethal overdose" of tobacco. To the extent that tobacco causes deaths, it does so through the cumulative effects of smoking tobacco-filled cigarettes, cigars, and pipes. Unless Lowry intends to deny that most marijuana users get high through smoking it and that they usually do so without the filters commonly attached to cigarettes, one must assume that marijuana is at least as lethal as tobacco. As for alcohol, while it, unlike marijuana, can cause death when taken in extremely large doses, the same could also be said for such legal substances as aspirin. That it is possible for a drug to be taken in lethal quantities is, then, insufficient to determine whether it is harmful enough to be outlawed.

The Gateway Argument

Much more potent is Lowry's argument against the conventional wisdom that pot is a "gateway drug" to such "harder" substances as LSD, cocaine, methamphetamine, and heroin. Reversing accepted assumptions, Lowry denies both that kids who use marijuana go on to experiment with stronger drugs and that those who do so are led to this behavior by the marijuana itself. As he points out, just "because a cocaine addict used marijuana first doesn't mean he is on cocaine because he smoked marijuana." To argue in this way is, he claims, to confuse "temporality with causality." It is more likely that children who experiment with drugs of all kinds do so because of a preexisting behavioral problem. It's thus "the kid, not the substance, who is the problem."

Like the National Rifle Association's effective campaign to persuade the country that "guns don't kill people, people kill people," Lowry's argument contains much truth. Of course a troubled child is more likely to try drugs than one with a firm sense of right and wrong. But that's far from being the end of the story. Just as a would-be murderer can usually do far more harm with a gun than he could with a less potent weapon, so a child in danger of losing his way can do more damage to himself when drugs are widely available for his use, as they surely would be if they were legalized.

And then there is the question of education. The behavioral problems that Lowry points to as the true cause of drug abuse do not arise in a vacuum. They come about largely from a failure of moral education—by schools, but much more so by parents. As it is, the law provides a small but significant amount of support for parents in their efforts to steer their kids away from drugs. Libertarians may argue that legalization would not undermine those efforts—that it would merely leave it up to individuals to decide for themselves—but as opponents of the unlimited abortion license are well aware, legal neutrality is often far from neutral. When we outlaw some actions (like murder) and permit others (like abortion) we make a crucially important distinction. We teach that the former are unambiguously wrong and that the latter are not. To legalize marijuana is thus to weaken the position of parents who wish to steel their children against the temptation of drug-taking.

But Lowry nevertheless has a point. If it is true that few users of marijuana become users of other drugs, then the rationale for keeping pot illegal has indeed been undermined. Add to this the scientifically established fact that, unlike alcohol, nicotine, and cocaine, marijuana is not physically addictive, and we cannot help but wonder if we should conclude, with Lowry, that marijuana is relatively harmless, and thus that punishing people for using it is "outrageously disproportionate."

The Pursuit of Pleasure

In two . . . columns for the *New Republic*, Andrew Sullivan goes beyond Lowry's position to declare flatly that "the illegal thing in pot is not THC [its active ingredient]; it's pleasure." And this, he claims, is absurd. In a country that increasingly medicates itself with pharmaceuticals, which, like pot, induce pleasure by manipulating chemicals already present in the human body, criminalizing the use and cultivation of marijuana appears to be completely arbitrary. In fact, according to Sullivan, it is only a "residual cultural puritanism" that stands in the way of allowing Americans to pursue "enjoyment" however they wish. "It is bizarre," he writes, "that, in a country founded in part on the pursuit of happiness, we should now be expending so many resources on incarcerating and terrorizing so many people simply because they are doing what their Constitution promised." Sure, he admits, "pleasure isn't the same thing as happiness." But "the responsible, adult enjoyment of . . . pleasure . . . is surely part of it."

The argument is a powerful one. If, in the end, the dispute about legalizing marijuana can be reduced to a conflict between those who support pleasure and those who oppose it, then the prohibitionists have already lost the argument. The Puritans simply won't be winning any elections in twenty-first century America. Nevertheless, we have reason to think that a case against legalization can be based on a less exacting distinction. That is, we can insist on distinguishing among kinds of pleasure, something that, common sense notwithstanding, Lowry and Sullivan each steadfastly refuse to do.

While most people believe that pleasure is a good thing, they also categorize and rank its different types. Some pleasures are subtle, others are intense. Some are best experienced alone, others can be enjoyed only in community. Some are base, others noble. Some are purely physical, while others are inextricably bound up with our higher powers. And then there are those most fulfilling pleasures—the ones that follow from the completion of the higher human endeavors. The late Allan Bloom noted the occasions that tend to elicit such feelings: "victory in a just war, consummated love, artistic creation, religious devotion, and the discovery of truth."

What Are Some Consequences of Marijuana Use?

- May cause frequent respiratory infections, impaired memory and learning, increased heart rate, anxiety, panic attacks, tolerance, and physical dependence.

- Use of marijuana during the first month of breast-feeding can impair infant motor development.

- Chronic smokers may have many of the same respiratory problems as tobacco smokers including daily cough and phlegm, chronic bronchitis symptoms, frequent chest colds; chronic abuse can also lead to abnormal functioning of lung tissues.

- A study of college students has shown that skills related to attention, memory, and learning are impaired among people who use marijuana heavily, even after discontinuing its use for at least 24 hours.

Drug Enforcement Administration, "Marijuana," 2002.

The pleasure of smoking marijuana differs from the kind of pleasure that accompanies smoking a fine cigar or sipping a well-brewed cup of coffee, and more pertinently, it also differs from the pleasure of mild drunkenness. Whereas alcohol primarily diminishes one's inhibitions and clarity of thought, marijuana inspires a euphoria that resembles nothing so much as the pleasure that normally arises only in response to the accomplishment of the noblest human deeds. Marijuana, like the designer drug Ecstasy, whose legalization Sullivan also, revealingly, supports, provides its users with a means to enjoy the rewards of excellence without possessing it themselves. Bloom again: "Without effort, without talent, without virtue, without exercise of the faculties, anyone and everyone is accorded the equal right to the enjoyment of their fruits."

The Difference Between Pleasure and Happiness

A country that consumes ever-greater doses of mood-altering prescription drugs might not deem this to be a significant problem, but it should. The danger is not merely that seeking happiness through pharmacology cuts us off from the world as it truly is. It is also that the very attempt to reach happiness in such a way must ultimately fail. While Sullivan is right to remark on the distinction between pleasure and happiness, he neglects to follow up on his insight—to think through what it is that separates them. If he had done so, he would have noted that, whereas pleasure involves enjoying something good, happiness arises only when we judge ourselves worthy of enjoying it.

This is why such actions as a just military victory can produce happiness, while inhaling marijuana smoke, however pleasurable, can lead only to an ersatz satisfaction—because it involves nothing praiseworthy. Thus it is that, after its effects have worn off, marijuana leaves its users with little more than a feeling of emptiness and a craving for another high to fill it. Hence also the unproductive stupor into which "potheads" frequently fall.

Lowry and Sullivan may be right to claim that marijuana does not lead to physical harm. But it does produce a pathology of the soul. And given the many pathogens that already pollute our culture—as well as our society's salutary prejudice against marijuana—that is reason enough to resist the efforts of some to remove the legal obstacles to getting high.

II

If you're looking for a good pot party on the right . . . , check out the pages of *National Review*.

Legalization of marijuana is founder William F. Buckley Jr.'s pet cause. (Mr. Common Touch has admitted to toking on his yacht in international waters.) Senior Editor Richard Brookhiser thinks marijuana is medicine. In the Aug. 20 [2001] issue, Editor-in-Chief Richard Lowry weighs in with "Weed Whackers—The Anti-Marijuana Forces and Why They're Wrong."

The article reads like a memo from the desk of George

Soros, the legalization movement's sugar daddy. Lowry writes, "Marijuana is widely used, and for the vast majority of its users is nearly harmless and represents a temporary experiment or enthusiasm."

He snorts at the gateway theory—that pot leads to more potent narcotics. "Since marijuana is the most widely used and least dangerous illegal drug, it makes sense that people *inclined to use* harder-to-find drugs will start with it first."

It's not that the high from marijuana disposes users to seek more intense experiences. For Lowry, inclination exists in a vacuum.

When legalization skeptics note that roughly 100,000 enter rehab programs for marijuana each year, Lowry counters that most are ordered into the programs by the courts, as punishment for possession.

And who orders them to go to emergency rooms? According to the University of Maryland's Center for Substance Abuse Research, in 1999, marijuana accounted for 79,088 emergency-room visits, slightly more than heroin.

A Direct Relationship Between Pot and Behavior

In 1998, 60 percent of juvenile arrestees in the District of Columbia tested positive for pot.

Here again, Lowry reverses cause and effect Teens don't get into trouble using marijuana, he insists. Troubled youth are attracted to the weed, it being one more way to rebel.

But parent after parent has told me: "My kid was normal (studious, well-behaved) until he started smoking pot. Then his personality changed overnight."

Analyzing data collected from 1994 to 1996, the National Household Surveys on Drug Abuse found a direct relationship between marijuana use and "delinquent/depressive behavior."

Of those who used marijuana one to 11 times in the previous year, 7 percent were on probation, compared to 20 percent who used it at least weekly.

The behavior tracked included "ran away from home," "physically attacked people" and "thought about suicide." In each instance, percentages involved in pathological behavior went up as frequency of use increased. Lowry doubtless would say it's coincidental—that moderately troubled teens are somewhat attracted to pot and very troubled teens are very attracted.

The Dutch Experience

He claims the Dutch experiment with decriminalization shows just how nearly harmless the weed is. According to one of the drug-lobby sources he quotes, "Removing the prohibition against possession does not increase cannabis use."

Actually, the Dutch experience refutes this. In the early '80s, Holland decriminalized possession of small quantities of the drug. Now, over 800 coffeehouses are licensed to sell various cannabis products.

In a May 9 [2001] editorial, the *Wall Street Journal* reported the nation saw a 250 percent increase in adolescent pot use following legalization. Between 1991 and 1996, the Dutch Ministry of Justice reported a 25 percent rise in violent crime, at a time when crime rates fell in the United States.

The Dutch wish someone would wake them from the nightmare. In a poll by Eramus University in Rotterdam, 61 percent said all drugs should be illegal and 75 percent disagreed with the police policy of only arresting addicts when they cause a public nuisance.

Why are some conservatives, like the *National Review* crowd, taking the magical mystery tour?

Beating the drums for legalization makes them look cool— or so they think. It's a way of gaining acceptance in a culture whose institutions are controlled by the '60s generation.

In its first issue, the editors of *National Review* said they intended to stand athwart the course of history, shouting, "Halt." Now, they're standing there with a joint in one hand, a copy of *High Times* in the other and a Beavis and Butthead grin, asking, "Heh, heh, what's happin', man?"

*"Because of prohibition, millions of people
are suffering needless pain, wasting away
because they are unable to eat, or
struggling to live while doped up on
dangerous, addictive synthetic drugs."*

Marijuana Should Be Legalized for Medical Use

Ed Rosenthal and Steve Kubby

Ed Rosenthal and Steve Kubby are the authors of the book *Why Marijuana Should Be Legal*, from which this viewpoint is excerpted. They argue that marijuana is effective at relieving pain, controlling nausea, and stimulating the appetite, and is successfully used to treat a large number of medical problems, including asthma, AIDS, depression, and glaucoma. Marinol, a synthetic formulation of THC—the chemical in marijuana that is responsible for many of its soothing effects—is not nearly as effective as natural marijuana, they claim. Millions of people are suffering needlessly because of the prohibition against using medical marijuana, Rosenthal and Kubby assert. They conclude that marijuana should be decriminalized.

As you read, consider the following questions:

1. What is the difference between Schedule I and Schedule II drugs, as cited by the authors?
2. What were the Institute of Medicine's findings about marijuana and medicine, as cited by Rosenthal and Kubby?
3. What are the major shortcomings of Marinol, according to Dr. Tod Mikuriya?

Ed Rosenthal and Steve Kubby, *Why Marijuana Should Be Legal*. New York: Thunder's Mouth Press, 2003. Copyright © 1996 by Ed Rosenthal and Steve Kubby. All rights reserved. Reproduced by permission.

Nearly all medicines have toxic, potentially lethal effects. But marijuana is not such a substance. There is no record in the extensive medical literature describing a proven, documented cannabis-induced fatality. . . . Marijuana, in its natural form, is one of the safest therapeutically active substances known to man.

Drug Enforcement Administration
Administrative Law Judge Francis L. Young

Of all the reasons to legalize marijuana, none is more compelling than its medical usage. Marijuana has a wide variety of therapeutic applications, and is frequently beneficial in treating the following conditions:

- *AIDS.* Marijuana reduces the nausea, vomiting, and loss of appetite caused by both the ailment itself and as a side effect of treatment with AZT and other medicines.
- *Asthma.* Several studies have shown that THC [the active ingredient in marijuana] acts as a bronchodilator and reverses bronchial constriction. Although conventional bronchodilators work faster than marijuana, THC has been shown to last longer and with considerably less risk.
- *Arthritis and Other Autoimmune Diseases.* In addition to its effectiveness in controlling the pain associated with arthritis, new evidence shows that marijuana is an autoimmune modulator.
- *Cancer.* Marijuana stimulates the appetite and alleviates nausea and vomiting, common side effects of chemotherapy treatment. People undergoing chemotherapy find that smoking marijuana is an antinauseant often more effective than mainstream medications.
- *Chronic Pain.* Marijuana alleviates the debilitating, chronic pain caused by myriad disorders and injuries.
- *Depression and Other Mood Disorders.* Marijuana has been shown to help dysphoria gently and naturally. Conventional antidepressant and mood-stabilizing drugs like selective serotonin reuptake inhibitors (e.g., Prozac, Zoloft, etc.), lithium, tricyclics, and MAO inhibitors have serious health risks and side effects.
- *Epilepsy.* Marijuana is used as an adjunctive medicine to prevent epileptic seizures. Some patients find that they

can reduce dosage of other seizure-control medications while using cannabis.

- *Glaucoma.* Marijuana can reduce intraocular pressure, alleviating pain and slowing (and sometimes stopping) the progress of the condition.
- *Menstrual Cramps and Labor Pain.* Many women use pot to ease the pain of menstrual cramps and childbirth, but don't disclose their behavior for fear their babies will be taken away from them. Women who use marijuana for labor and delivery report that it is far more effective pain relief than conventional drugs, and that their babies are more alert at birth. One study of such marijuana babies showed that children of moderate smokers show superior psychomotor skills.
- *Multiple Sclerosis.* Marijuana limits the muscle pain and spasticity caused by the disease, and relieves tremor and unsteady gait. (Multiple sclerosis is the leading cause of neurological disability among young and middle-aged adults in the United States, and strikes two to three times more women than men.)
- *Muscle Spasm and Spasticity.* Medical marijuana has been clinically shown to be effective in relieving these.
- *Migraine Headaches.* Marijuana not only relieves pain, but also inhibits the release of serotonin during attacks.
- *Paraplegia and Quadriplegia.* Many paraplegics and quadriplegics have discovered that cannabis not only relieves their pain more safely than opiates, but also suppresses their muscle twitches and tremors.
- *Pruritis (Itching).* Marijuana can be used orally and topically for this condition and may be more effective than corticosteroids and antihistamines.
- *Insomnia.* Research shows pot can help people sleep—without the side effects or tolerance problems of other hypnotics. Cannabidiol is the active ingredient in pot that induces sleep.

In 1988, Judge Francis Young of the DEA [Drug Enforcement Administration] found marijuana to be "the safest therapeutic substance known to man" and urged its reclassification and distribution for medical uses. Jon Gettman, NORML [National Organization for the Reform of Mari-

DEA Federal Drug Scheduling Guidelines

	Schedule I	Schedule II
SUBSTANCES	Marijuana, LSD, Heroin, Quaaludes	Amphetamines, Cocaine, Codeine, Morphine, Methadone, Opium, PCP
POTENTIAL FOR ABUSE	High potential for abuse	High potential for abuse
MEDICAL USE	No currently accepted medical use in treatment in the U.S.	Medical use in treatment currently accepted in the U.S., possibly with severe restrictions
LIKELIHOOD OF DEPENDENCE	There is no safe acceptable use even under medical supervision	Abuse may lead to severe psychological or physical dependence

juana Laws] director from 1986 to 1989, filed a petition to reschedule marijuana in 1995. Gettman contended that marijuana should be rescheduled from a Schedule I to a Schedule II drug, since it fails to meet the legal criteria for Schedule I classification, which is the most restrictive category under the Controlled Substances Act. Both Schedule I and Schedule II drugs are substances with "a high potential for abuse." The difference is that Schedule I drugs "have no currently accepted medical application in the U.S.," while Schedule II drugs, such as morphine, cocaine, and PCP, can be prescribed for a currently accepted medical use. The Federal Drug Administration (FDA) advised against a reclassification in 2001. On May 24, 2002, the United States Court of Appeals for the District of Columbia ruled to uphold the DEA's determination, maintaining marijuana's Schedule I status.

In 1999, the Institute of Medicine, a branch of the Na-

Schedule III	Schedule IV	Schedule V
Marinol, Anabolic Steroids, Barbiturates, Phenobarbital	Xanax, Valium, Halcion, Ambien	Robitussin A–C, Lomotil
Moderate potential for abuse (lower potential than substances in Schedules I or II)	Low potential for abuse (lower potential than substances in Schedules III)	Lowest potential for abuse (lower potential than substances in Schedules IV)
Medical use in treatment currently accepted in the U.S.	Medical use in treatment currently accepted in the U.S.	Medical use in treatment currently accepted in the U.S.
Abuse may lead to moderate or low physical dependence or high psychological dependence	Abuse may lead to limited physical dependence or psychological dependence	Abuse may lead to limited physical dependence or psychological dependence

Ed Rosenthal and Steve Kubby, *Why Marijuana Should Be Legal*. New York: Thunder's Mouth Press, 2003.

tional Academy of Sciences (NAS), issued a report titled *Marijuana and Medicine: Assessing the Science Base.* Among the findings of this committee of medical experts: "The accumulated data indicate a potential therapeutic value for cannabinoid drugs, particularly for symptoms such as pain relief, control of nausea and vomiting, and appetite stimulation." While they were cautionary about smoked marijuana as medicine, they acknowledged that people suffering from some chronic conditions have no clear alternative to smoked marijuana for pain relief. These judicial findings have been totally ignored by the DEA and other federal agencies.

After years of suppression by the government, the truth about medical marijuana is finally coming out. Dr. Tod Mikuriya, former director of marijuana research for the entire federal government, explains: "I was hired by the government to provide scientific evidence that marijuana was harmful. As

I studied the subject, I began to realize that marijuana was once widely used as a safe and effective medicine. But the government had a different agenda, and I had to resign."

From 1994 until 1996, Mikuriya spent much of his time studying patients who were receiving medical marijuana under the auspices of the San Francisco Cannabis Buyers' Club. (In July 1996, the club was closed by court order at the instigation of California Attorney General Dan Lundgren.) Mikuriya has continued his work with patients since then. Eventually the dispensary reopened, only to be closed again by the federal government in 2000. He is currently medical coordinator of the California Cannabis Centers and a member of the city of Oakland's Medical Marijuana Work Group.

In February 1994, Dennis Peron and friends founded the Buyers' Club and began openly selling cannabis to people with HIV, cancer, intractable pain, and multiple sclerosis. Their daring actions, which they called "compassionate use," were serious violations of federal law, but Peron and his group were determined to provide sick people with an herb that could help them gain weight and cope with pain. Fortunately, the city of San Francisco was squarely on their side.

Medical authorities such as Dr. DuPont of NIMH [National Institute of Mental Health] have claimed that marijuana will never be accepted as a medicine because dosages can't be controlled. This is not necessarily the case, for patients report that they control dosages when they smoke. One patient summarized a prevailing opinion among his peers: "Doctors hate the idea of patients self-medicating . . . but we patients know our bodies, and we can do a better job than doctors at judging when we've reached an effective dosage."

It is true that smoked marijuana is very fast acting, so it is easy for an experienced patient to regulate his or her dose. In addition, more patients are using tinctures, foods, and pills to standardize dosage.

Problems with Marinol

DuPont also insists that regular marijuana is dangerous, and that patients should receive their treatments in the form of capsulized Marinol. Generically known as dronabinol, Marinol is a highly concentrated synthetic formulation of delta-

9-THC, one of the active forms of THC found in natural marijuana.

Dr. Mikuriya strongly disagrees. "There are over twenty active forms of THC and over sixty different cannabinoids which are active in marijuana. Marinol contains only one form of THC and no other cannabinoids, so it's just part of the answer." It's an expensive prescription drug, at $10 or more per capsule. When used as recommended, it costs $80 a day, or up to $1,000 a week. In comparison, natural marijuana can be grown inexpensively.

So far, nine states and the District of Columbia have recognized this and legalized growing and/or possession of marijuana by patients or their caregivers; however, federal laws continue to make growing under any circumstance a crime.

Other Shortcomings

Marinol has two other major shortcomings:

- Because it contains pure THC, it packs a powerful wallop that many patients find unpleasant and even incapacitating. Natural marijuana contains many other nonpsychoactive ingredients with medical actions of their own that can counteract the adverse effect of THC.
- In patients suffering from nausea, swallowing capsules may itself provoke vomiting. In 2002, Dr. Notcutt reported results of human testing for pain relief in MS patients. Neither THC nor CBD was effective alone as an analgesic. However, when combined, they were extremely efficacious.

Many patients and physicians avoid Marinol because they have found that smoking natural marijuana delivers THC more efficiently and allows them to continue their normal activities. Dennis Peron is even more adamant: "Marinol costs up to $35,000 a year and doesn't work. Our patients at the Buyers' Club who have tried it say it made them so stoned they couldn't function or that it had other adverse effects. Also, Marinol is a pill, so you have to keep it down long enough to help the nausea. That's nuts, and it doesn't work."

The continuing prohibition of medical marijuana is based more on political than scientific considerations. Although during the 1970s the government supported exploration into marijuana's therapeutic potential, it has now taken on the role of blocking new research and opposing any change in marijuana's legal status. Agencies such as NIMH have steadfastly refused to allow investigations into the benefits of marijuana.

More than twenty states have passed legislation to allow marijuana's use as a medicine, but federal law preempts these statutes. Although the feds insist that marijuana has no medical benefits, there is ample evidence that medical marijuana works:

- Forty-four percent of oncologists responding to a questionnaire said they had recommended marijuana to their cancer patients. Fifty-four percent said they would recommend medical marijuana if it were legal.
- Several studies have clearly shown that marijuana is effective in reducing nausea and vomiting.
- Patients undergoing cancer chemotherapy have found smoking marijuana to be more effective than available pharmaceutical medications, including Marinol.
- Marijuana is also smoked by thousands of AIDS patients to treat the symptoms associated with both the disease and drug therapy. Because it stimulates appetite, marijuana also counters HIV-related "wasting," allowing AIDS patients to gain weight and prolong their lives.

Because of prohibition, millions of people are suffering needless pain, wasting away because they are unable to eat, or struggling to live while doped up on dangerous, addictive synthetic drugs. Marijuana decriminalization can give these unfortunate people a natural, inexpensive herb to relieve their pain, while restoring their appetite and their enjoyment of life. . . .

A Terrible Price to Pay

Marijuana prohibition has caused us to pay a terrible price in pain and suffering, especially for those who are critically ill and might otherwise benefit from this unique herbal medicine. The drug warriors assure us that "marijuana has no medical uses," but the truth is that as long as marijuana is illegal, all of us are being denied a valuable medicine which can provide nontoxic, long-lasting relief, and even cures for a host of common ailments.

"[Marijuana] has not been scientifically proven safe and effective. . . . Under federal law, there is really no basis to distinguish "medical" marijuana trafficking from marijuana trafficking generally."

Marijuana Should Not Be Legalized for Medical Use

Laura M. Nagel

Laura M. Nagel is the deputy assistant administrator in the office of Diversion Control of the Drug Enforcement Administration. She argues in the following viewpoint, which was originally given as testimony before the House Subcommittee on Criminal Justice, Drug Policy, and Human Resources in March 2001, that marijuana has not been proven safe and effective as a drug to treat medical conditions. Therefore, she contends, it should not be legalized for "medicinal" purposes. Moreover, she claims, several cannabis clubs that have been established to sell "medical" marijuana are actually fronts for drug trafficking. "Medical" marijuana initiatives are thinly disguised attempts to legalize marijuana.

As you read, consider the following questions:
1. What factors are taken into consideration when determining in which schedule a drug should be placed, according to Nagel?
2. What example does Nagel provide to illustrate how marijuana trafficking is occurring under the guise of dispensing medicine?

Laura M. Nagel, testimony before the House Committee on Government Reform, Subcommittee on Criminal Justice, Drug Policy, and Human Resources, March 27, 2001.

L et me begin with a discussion of the Controlled Substances Act (CSA) and the scheduling process. The CSA, Title II of the Comprehensive Drug Abuse Prevention and Control Act of 1970, is the legal foundation for the United States' fight against abuse of drugs and other substances. The CSA was passed to minimize the quantity of abuseable substances available to those likely to abuse them, while providing for legitimate medical, scientific and industrial needs of those substances in the United States. The Drug Enforcement Administration (DEA) is the agency within the Department of Justice primarily responsible for the administration and enforcement of the provisions of the CSA.

The Controlled Substance Act

The CSA places substances with a substantial potential for abuse into one of five schedules. Both legitimately produced drugs and clandestinely manufactured substances are included in the list of substances controlled under the CSA. This placement is based on the substance's accepted medical use, safety, potential for abuse, and/or dependence liability; Schedule I is the most restrictive and Schedule V is the least restrictive schedule. The Act also provides a mechanism for (1) substances to be controlled or added to a schedule, (2) decontrolled or removed from a schedule, and (3) rescheduled or transferred from one schedule to another. Proceedings to add, change, or remove a substance from the schedules listed in the CSA can be initiated either (1) by the Attorney General or Administrator of DEA (after reports from DEA field offices, state control authorities, treatment clinics, or other sources regarding the diversion or abuse problems associated with a substance), (2) at the request of the Secretary of Health and Human Services (HHS), or (3) by petition from any interested party (including a pharmaceutical company, advocacy group, or private citizen). . . .

Criteria for the Schedules

For Schedule I substances, the criteria that need to be considered are whether the substance has a high potential for abuse, has no currently accepted medical use in treatment in the United States, and has a lack of accepted safety for use under medical supervision.

For substances in Schedule II, the criteria that need to be considered are its high potential for abuse, whether it has a currently accepted medical use in treatment in the United States or a currently accepted medical use with severe restrictions and whether abuse of the substances may lead to severe psychological or physical dependence.

A substance is placed in one of Schedules III through V based on its potential for abuse relative to substances in other schedules, whether it has a currently accepted medical use in treatment in the United States, and its relative potential to produce physical or psychological dependence. . . .

It should be noted that the majority of controlled substances are in Schedules II through V. Some drug substances were placed in Schedule I by Congress in 1970 and others added in subsequent years because of their high potential for abuse and lack of medical safety and use in the United States. These actions have withstood the test of time and scientific scrutiny and remain there today. These control actions have saved an indeterminable number of lives within the United States. However, the CSA has proved to be a dynamic law that has allowed for the evolution of science and technology to progress to the point in which some Schedule I substances have been developed for medical use and the CSA has been modified from its original listings to bring new drug products to the general medical community.

"Medical" Marijuana

I would now like to address the impact state laws such as California's Proposition 215 have had on federal law enforcement. These state laws purport to legalize marijuana for "medical" use. These so-called "medical marijuana laws" work as follows: If a doctor "recommends" that a patient use marijuana for any ailment, then it is legal for the patient to grow and use marijuana. At present, Alaska, California, Colorado, Hawaii, Maine, Nevada, Oregon, and Washington have passed such laws. Arizona has passed a law that allows doctors to prescribe any Schedule I drug. Contrary to these laws, marijuana remains an illegal drug under federal law.

Actually "medical" marijuana is actually a misnomer since marijuana is in fact a Schedule I drug. As such, it has not been scientifically proven safe and effective in accordance with the Food, Drug, and Cosmetic Act and cannot be used except in research approved by the FDA [Food and Drug Administration] and registered with DEA. Under federal law, there is really no basis to distinguish "medical" marijuana trafficking from marijuana trafficking generally.

Marijuana Is a Very Unpredictable "Medicine"

John Malouf, a spokesman for Australian Pharmacists Against Drug Abuse, stated, "Cannabis sativa must be one of the most controversial drugs of all time. Botanically it is a very unstable species with over a hundred plant varieties of differing strengths. . . . This basic botanical fact has been ignored by many who discuss the drug as if it were a single substance with mild intoxicant properties. Its unpredictable nature varies immensely from individual to individual and according to the strength of the product used."

Robert L. Maginnis, "Marijuana Is Bad Medicine: 2001 Update," www.frc. org, 2001.

Historically, DEA has directed its investigative resources at major trafficking organizations without regard to whether the traffickers might claim to have a "medical" excuse for violating the law. This is not to say that these current state laws have not caused conflict and confusion throughout the law enforcement community. California's Attorney General publicly announced his unwillingness to enforce the state's drug laws against traffickers who claim to be involved with "medical" marijuana. He has left it to the individual counties and municipalities to arrive at their own criteria for implementation of Proposition 215. The California localities that have taken a public position on Proposition 215 have issued vague guidelines, all of which send a clear message that anyone who has a "recommendation" from a doctor is permitted to grow and possess certain amounts of marijuana. The City of Oakland for example allows each person to possess up to six pounds of marijuana. Since there is a complete lack of state government oversight, each grower is on his or her honor not to exceed these vague guidelines.

California has now become the home of several "cannabis" clubs that openly distribute marijuana to anyone who the club owners decide has a "medical" need for the drug. In some jurisdictions, local sheriffs have given groups advance permission to grow marijuana while state judges have ordered law enforcement officials to return marijuana seized from criminal defendants who claim to be handling the drug for "medical" reasons. Even where local police have made arrests and seizures, there have been numerous instances where local district attorneys have been unwilling to prosecute because the defendants supposedly complied with the "spirit" of Proposition 215.

Marijuana Trafficking

An example of how marijuana trafficking is occurring under the guise of medicine is illustrated in one particular case in 1999. A local television station in New Orleans informed law enforcement officials that it had discovered an Internet web site advertising the sale of "medical" marijuana. The web site was established by an individual who distributed marijuana from his home in Anaheim, California. After the United States Attorney's Office for the Eastern District of Louisiana advised DEA that it would prosecute the case, DEA undercover agents placed orders which resulted in marijuana being shipped to the agents in New Orleans. In September 1999, agents from the DEA and IRS [Internal Revenue Service] together with the Anaheim Police Department executed a search warrant at the defendant's home. During the execution of the warrant, the defendant advised that he had been selling "medical" marijuana for nearly three years. Records revealed that he had distributed more than 50 pounds to 149 different customers in 35 different states. On February 11, 2000, the defendant was indicted by a federal grand jury in New Orleans on charges of distribution of marijuana and advertising the distribution of a Schedule I controlled substance. During the execution of the search warrant, agents also seized numerous "recommendation" letters that appear to have been issued by doctors in various states to customers.

The resulting dilemma has been further viewed as jeopardizing the historical cooperation between federal, state, and local drug enforcement officials. For example, local officers assigned to a federally funded task force might find themselves in the situation of having to seize marijuana in order to enforce federal law, knowing that the local prosecutor will refuse to prosecute or the local judge will order the marijuana returned to the grower. In essence, allowing traffickers to carry on with impunity in this manner simply undercuts enforcement of the Controlled Substances Act and allows an unproven and potentially dangerous drug to be sold to the public as "medicine".

Two pending lawsuits have developed from law enforcement efforts to keep this situation in check. In *United States vs. Oakland Cannabis Buyers' Cooperative* the U.S. sought an injunction ordering this "cannabis club" to stop growing and distributing marijuana in violation of federal law. The club claimed a "medical necessity" defense that allowed it to distribute marijuana. The Ninth Circuit Court of Appeals recognized that this was a legally cognizable defense. The United States Supreme Court will hear argument on this case on March 28th, 2001.[1] In *Conant vs. ONDCP, DOJ, DEA, and HHS* a group of Californians sued the Government claiming that doctors have a "free speech" right to "recommend" that their patients use marijuana in violation of federal law. The federal district court agreed and issued an injunction that prohibits DEA from investigating doctors who "recommend" marijuana or revoking their DEA registrations.

International Treaties

Lastly, I would like to point out that the United States is a party to several international treaties to control international and domestic traffic in controlled substances. These are expressly recognized by Congress in the Controlled Substances Act. Most notable are: the 1961 Single Convention on Narcotic Drugs; the 1971 Convention on Psychotropic Substances; and the 1988 Convention Against Illicit Traffic in Narcotic Drugs and Psychotropic Substances. Most of the

---

1. The Supreme Court ruled there is no medical necessity exception to the Controlled Substances Act.

provisions of the CSA must be in force in order for the United States to meet its obligations under these treaties. Treaty obligations that are relevant are as follows: the United States must enact and carry out legislation disallowing the use of Schedule I drugs outside of research; make it a criminal offense, subject to imprisonment, to traffic in illicit or to aid and abet such trafficking; and prohibit cultivation of marijuana except by persons licensed by, and under the direct supervision of the federal government.

There is no doubt that Proposition 215 and similar state initiatives provide an obstacle to the United States meeting its obligations under these treaties. In addition, allowing these state marijuana initiatives to remain in force potentially undermines diplomatic efforts by the United States to persuade other countries like Mexico and Colombia to enact and vigorously enforce their drug laws.

Periodical Bibliography

The following articles have been selected to supplement the diverse views presented in this chapter.

Dan P. Alsobrooks	"Waging a Battle Against the Myths," *Corrections Today*, December 2002.
Brian Bergman	"Just Say 'Yes': Legalizing Marijuana Would Actually Be Safer for Kids than Decriminalization," *Maclean's*, March 3, 2003.
Virginia Berridge	"Altered States: Opium and Tobacco Compared," *Social Research*, Fall 2001.
David Boyum and Mark A.R. Kleiman	"Breaking the Drug-Crime Link," *Public Interest*, Summer 2003.
Alexander Cockburn	"The Right Not to Be in Pain," *Nation*, February 3, 2003.
John DiConsiglio	"Hooked on Heroin," *Junior Scholastic*, April 25, 2003.
Luke Fisher	"Marijuana as Medicine," *Maclean's*, October 14, 2002.
Daniel Forbes	"Ashcroft's Other War," *Rolling Stone*, December 27, 2001.
Lester Grinspoon	"The Harmfulness Tax," *Social Research*, Fall 2001.
Johann Hari	"Just You Wait Until I Grow Up," *New Statesman*, July 9, 2001.
Asa Hutchinson	"Drug Legalization Doesn't Work," *Washington Post*, October 9, 2002.
Robert Maccoun and Peter Reuter	"Marijuana, Heroin, and Cocaine: The War on Drugs May Be a Disaster, but Do We Really Want a Legalized Peace?" *American Prospect*, June 3, 2002.
Barry McCaffrey	"We Have No 'War on Drugs,'" *World and I*, February 2000.
Sara Rimensnyder	"The Feds vs. Medical Pot: One Toke over the Line," *Reason*, March 2002.
Sue Rusche and Marsha Rosenbaum	"Do Efforts to Legalize Marijuana for Medical Use Encourage Teen Drug Use?" *CQ Researcher*, March 15, 2002.
Jacob Sullum	"H: The Surprising Truth About Heroin and Addiction," *Reason*, June 2003.
Jacob Sullum	"High Road: Is Marijuana a 'Gateway'?" *Reason*, March 2003.
John P. Walters	"Don't Legalize Drugs," *Wall Street Journal*, July 19, 2002.
Clare Wilson	"Fixed Up: When Nothing Else Works, Heroin Addicts Should Be Prescribed the Drug They Crave," *New Scientist*, March 30, 2002.

For Further Discussion

Chapter 1

1. Asa Hutchinson and Edmund F. McGarrell argue that the war on drugs is succeeding because the number of drug users has been drastically reduced in the past three decades. Matthew B. Stannard and Timothy Lynch contend that the demand for illegal drugs is still strong. Based on your reading of the viewpoints, do you think the war on drugs will ever be able to completely eliminate the demand for illegal drugs? If not, should the government continue its efforts to combat drug abuse? Why or why not?

2. Deborah Small asserts that blacks represent a disproportionate number of prison inmates because the criminal justice system makes and enforces drug laws in ways that discriminate against blacks. According to Heather MacDonald, however, using a suspect's race—along with other factors—can provide useful information for police officers who are looking for drug offenders. Do you think minorities are unfairly targeted by U.S. drug laws? Support your answer.

3. Joseph D. McNamara contends that the war on drugs tempts police officers to falsify evidence to ensure that drug offenders are convicted and sentenced to long terms in prison. Do you think the end result of imprisoning dangerous and violent drug dealers justifies using possibly illegal law enforcement tactics? Explain.

Chapter 2

1. Both Asa Hutchinson and Eugene Oscapella argue that profits from illegal drugs are used to support terrorists and their illegal activities. However, the authors reach opposite conclusions about why this is so and what should be done to stop it. Which author is more persuasive? Why?

2. Both Robert Novak and Eric E. Sterling agree that terrorist groups pose a threat to the United States, but they differ on how the war on terror should be fought. Based on your reading of the viewpoints, whose argument do you find more convincing? Why?

Chapter 3

1. David Risley, an assistant U.S. attorney, argues that mandatory minimum sentences for drug offenders are necessary to ensure that convicted drug dealers receive equal and fair punishments. Julie Stewart founded the organization Families Against Mandatory Minimums after her brother was convicted and sentenced to prison for growing marijuana. She thinks his sentence was

unjust. How does knowledge about each author's background affect your evaluation of their arguments?

2. Paul Armentano argues that the drug education program, Drug Abuse Resistance Education (DARE), is ineffective in preventing drug use among children. He cites studies that show little difference in drug use between children who have participated in DARE programs and those who have not. Tim Schennum maintains, however, that any program that teaches children how to resist peer pressure and avoid violence is worthwhile. Do you accept Armentano's criticism of DARE, or do you believe that Schennum's argument has more merit? Explain.

Chapter 4

1. One problem faced by proponents of drug legalization is that of defining exactly what legalization would mean in practice. Some authors in this chapter advocate legalization, but with restrictions similar to those placed on the purchase and use of alcohol and tobacco. What are the arguments against this position? Would legalizing drugs, but placing restrictions on who can buy them, be effective in reducing drug abuse or would it encourage more people to use drugs? Defend your answer with references to the viewpoints.

2. Bruce Anderson, Andrew Sullivan, and Rich Lowry contend that many illegal drugs are not as physically harmful as they are portrayed to be. Katie Grant, Damon Linker, and Don Feder argue, however, that legalization of such drugs would lead to increased drug abuse and addiction, particularly among children. In your opinion, should these substances be legalized? Explain.

3. Ed Rosenthal and Steve Kubby assert that smoked marijuana provides medical benefits that no other drug can match. Laura M. Nagel disagrees, arguing that marijuana has not been proven to be safe or effective. Rosenthal and Kubby are both involved in cannabis clubs in California that provide marijuana to seriously ill people. Nagel works for the Drug Enforcement Administration, which is responsible for determining whether drugs should be legal or illegal. Do the authors' backgrounds influence your assessment of their arguments? Explain.

Organizations to Contact

The editors have compiled the following list of organizations concerned with the issues debated in this book. The descriptions are derived from materials provided by the organizations. All have publications or information available for interested readers. The list was compiled on the date of publication of the present volume; the information provided here may change. Be aware that many organizations take several weeks or longer to respond to inquiries, so allow as much time as possible.

American Civil Liberties Union (ACLU)
125 Broad St., 18th Fl., New York, NY 10004-2400
(212) 549-2500
e-mail: aclu@aclu.org • website: www.aclu.org
The ACLU is a national organization that works to defend Americans' civil rights guaranteed by the U.S. Constitution. It provides legal defense, research, and education. The ACLU opposes the criminal prohibition of marijuana and the civil liberties violations that result from it. Its publications include ACLU Briefing Paper No. 19: *Against Drug Prohibition* and *Ira Glasser on Marijuana Myths and Facts.*

American Council for Drug Education (ACDE)
164 W. 74th St., New York, NY 10023
(800) 488-DRUG (3784) • (212) 595-5810
fax: (212) 595-2553
website: www.acde.org
The American Council for Drug Education informs the public about the harmful effects of abusing drugs and alcohol. It gives the public access to scientifically based, compelling prevention programs and materials. ACDE has resources for parents, youth, educators, prevention professionals, employers, health care professionals, and other concerned community members who are working to help America's youth avoid the dangers of drug and alcohol abuse.

Canadian Centre on Substance Abuse (CCSA)
75 Albert St., Suite 300, Ottawa, ON K1P 5E7 CANADA
(613) 235-4048 • fax: (613) 235-8101
e-mail: admin@ccsa.ca • website: www.ccsa.ca
Established in 1988 by an Act of Parliament, CCSA works to minimize the harm associated with the use of alcohol, tobacco, and other drugs. It disseminates information on the nature, extent, and consequences of substance abuse; sponsors public debates on the

topic; and supports organizations involved in substance abuse treatment, prevention, and educational programming. The center publishes the newsletter *Action News* six times a year.

Canadian Foundation for Drug Policy (CFDP)
70 MacDonald St., Ottawa, ON K2P 1H6 CANADA
(613) 236-1027 • fax: (613) 238-2891
e-mail: eoscapel@cfdp.ca • website: www.cfdp.ca

Founded by several of Canada's leading drug policy specialists, CFDP examines the objectives and consequences of Canada's drug laws and policies, including laws prohibiting marijuana. When necessary, the foundation recommends alternatives that it believes would make Canada's drug policies more effective and humane. CFDP discusses drug policy issues with the Canadian government, media, and general public. It also disseminates educational materials and maintains a website.

Cato Institute
1000 Massachusetts Ave. NW, Washington, DC 20001-5403
(202) 842-0200
e-mail: cato@cato.org • website: www.cato.org

The institute is a public policy research foundation dedicated to limiting the control of government and to protecting individual liberty. Cato, which strongly favors drug legalization, publishes the *Cato Journal* three times a year and the *Cato Policy Report* bimonthly.

Committees of Correspondence
11 John St., Room 506, New York, NY 10038
(212) 233-7151 • fax: (212) 233-7063

The Committees of Correspondence is a national coalition of community groups that campaign against drug abuse among youth by publishing data about drugs and drug abuse. The coalition opposes drug legalization and advocates treatment for drug abusers. Its publications include the quarterly *Drug Abuse Newsletter*, the periodic *Drug Prevention Resource Manual*, and related pamphlets, brochures, and article reprints.

Drug Enforcement Administration (DEA)
700 Army Navy Dr., Arlington, VA 22202
(202) 307-1000
website: www.usdoj.gov/deahome.htm

The DEA is the federal agency charged with enforcing the nation's drug laws. The agency concentrates on stopping the smuggling and distribution of narcotics in the United States and abroad. It publishes the *Drug Enforcement Magazine* three times a year.

Drug Policy Foundation
4455 Connecticut Ave. NW, Suite B-500, Washington, DC 20008-2328
(202) 537-5005 • fax: (202) 537-3007
e-mail: dpf@dpf.org • website: www.dpf.org
The foundation, an independent nonprofit organization, supports and publicizes alternatives to current U.S. policies on illegal drugs, including marijuana. The foundation's publications include the bimonthly *Drug Policy Letter* and the book *The Great Drug War*. It also distributes *Press Clips*, an annual compilation of newspaper articles on drug legalization issues, as well as legislative updates.

Family Research Council
801 G St. NW, Washington, DC 20001
(202) 393-2100 • (800) 225-4008 • (202) 393-2134
e-mail: corrdept@frc.org • website: www.frc.org
The council analyzes issues affecting the family and seeks to ensure that the interests of the traditional family are considered in the formulation of public policy. It lobbies legislatures and promotes public debate on issues concerning the family. The council publishes articles and position papers against the legalization of medicinal marijuana.

Heritage Foundation
214 Massachusetts Ave. NE, Washington, DC 20002-2302
(202) 546-4400
The Heritage Foundation is a conservative public policy research institute that opposes the legalization of drugs and advocates strengthening law enforcement to stop drug abuse. It publishes position papers on a broad range of topics, including drug issues. Its regular publications include the monthly *Policy Review*, the Backgrounder series of occasional papers, and the Heritage Lecture series.

Lindesmith Center
400 W. 59th St., New York, NY 10019
(212) 548-0695 • fax: (212) 548-4670
e-mail: lindesmith@sorosny.org • website: www.lindesmith.org
The Lindesmith Center is a policy research institute that focuses on broadening the debate on drug policy and related issues. The center houses a library and information center; organizes seminars

and conferences; acts as a link between scholars, government, and the media; directs a grant program in Europe; and undertakes projects on drug policy topics, including medicinal marijuana. It addresses issues of drug policy reform through a variety of projects, including the Drug Policy Seminar series, the International Harm Reduction Development Program, and the Methadone Policy Reform Project. The center's website includes articles, polls, and legal documents relating to marijuana.

Marijuana Policy Project
PO Box 77492, Capitol Hill, Washington, DC 20013
(202) 462-5747 • fax: (202) 232-0442
e-mail: mpp@mpp.org • website: www.mpp.org
The Marijuana Policy Project develops and promotes policies to minimize the harm associated with marijuana. It is the only organization that is solely concerned with lobbying to reform the marijuana laws on the federal level. The project increases public awareness through speaking engagements, educational seminars, the mass media, and briefing papers.

Media Awareness Project (MAP)
PO Box 651, Porterville, CA 93258
(800) 266-5759
e-mail: mgreer@mapinc.org • website: www.mapinc.org
MAP is an international network of activists dedicated to drug policy reform, with an emphasis on impacting public opinion and media coverage of drug policy issues. It opposes the criminal justice/prosecution/interdiction model of drug policy and favors a more liberal approach. MAP publishes the weekly *DrugSense* newsletter and makes tens of thousands of drug policy-related articles available on its website.

Multidisciplinary Association for Psychedelic Studies (MAPS)
2121 Commonwealth Ave., Suite 220, Charlotte, NC 28205
(704) 334-1798 • fax: (704) 334-1799
e-mail: info@maps.org • website: www.maps.org
MAPS is a membership-based research and educational organization. It focuses on the development of beneficial, socially sanctioned uses of psychedelic drugs and marijuana. MAPS helps scientific researchers obtain governmental approval for, fund, conduct, and report on psychedelic research in human volunteers. It publishes the quarterly *MAPS Bulletin* as well as various reports and newsletters.

National Center on Addiction and Substance Abuse (CASA)
Columbia University, 152 W. 57th St., New York, NY 10019-3310
(212) 841-5200 • fax: (212) 956-8020
website: www.casacolumbia.org
CASA is a private nonprofit organization that works to educate the public about the hazards of chemical dependency. The organization supports treatment as the best way to reduce chemical dependency. It produces publications describing the harmful effects of alcohol and drug addiction and effective ways to address the problem of substance abuse.

National Clearinghouse for Alcohol and Drug Information
PO Box 2345, Rockville, MD 20847-2345
(800) 729-6686 • (301) 468-2600 • fax: (301) 468-6433
e-mail: shs@health.org • website: www.health.org
The clearinghouse distributes publications of the U.S. Department of Health and Human Services, the National Institute on Drug Abuse, and other federal agencies concerned with alcohol and drug abuse. Brochure titles include *Tips for Teens About Marijuana*.

National Institute on Drug Abuse (NIDA)
U.S. Department of Health and Human Services
5600 Fishers Ln., Rockville, MD 20857
(301) 443-6245
e-mail: Information@lists.nida.nih • website: www.nida.nih.gov
NIDA supports and conducts research on drug abuse—including the yearly Monitoring the Future Survey—to improve addiction prevention, treatment, and policy efforts. It publishes the bimonthly *NIDA Notes* newsletter, the periodic NIDA Capsules fact sheets, and a catalog of research reports and public education materials, such as *Marijuana: Facts for Teens* and *Marijuana: Facts Parents Need to Know*.

National Organization for the Reform of Marijuana Laws (NORML)
1001 Connecticut Ave. NW, Suite 710, Washington, DC 20036
(202) 483-5500 • fax: (202) 483-0057
e-mail: natlnorml@aol.com • website: www.norml.org
NORML fights to legalize marijuana and to help those who have been convicted and sentenced for possessing or selling marijuana. In addition to pamphlets and position papers, it publishes the newsletter *Marijuana Highpoints*, the bimonthly *Legislative Bulletin* and *Freedom@NORML*, and the monthly *Potpourri*.

NORML Canada
c/o John W. Conroy
2459 Pauline St., Abbotsford, BC CANADA V2S 3S1
(604) 852-5110 • fax: (604) 859-3361
e-mail: jconroy@johnconroy.com
website: www.normlcanada.org

NORML Canada believes the discouragement of marijuana through use of criminal law has been excessively costly and harmful to both society and individuals. Although it does not advocate or encourage the use of marijuana, NORML Canada works at all levels of government to eliminate criminal penalties for private marijuana use.

Office of National Drug Control Policy
Drug Policy Information Clearinghouse
PO Box 6000, Rockville, MD 20849-6000
e-mail: ondcp@ncjrs.org
website: www.whitehousedrugpolicy.gov

The Office of National Drug Control Policy is responsible for formulating the government's national drug strategy and the president's antidrug policy as well as coordinating the federal agencies responsible for stopping drug trafficking. Drug policy studies are available upon request.

Partnership for a Drug-Free America
405 Lexington Ave., Suite 1601, New York, NY 10174
(212) 922-1560 • fax: (212) 922-1570
website: www.drugfreeamerica.org

The Partnership for a Drug-Free America is a nonprofit organization that utilizes media communication to reduce demand for illicit drugs in America. Best known for its national antidrug advertising campaign, the partnership works to "unsell" drugs to children and to prevent drug use among kids. It publishes the annual Partnership newsletter as well as monthly press releases about current events with which the partnership is involved.

Bibliography of Books

Rachel Green Baldino *Welcome to Methadonia: A Social Worker's Candid Account of Life in a Methadone Clinic.* Harrisburg, PA: White Hat Communications, 2001.

Alan Bock *Waiting to Inhale: The Politics of Medical Marijuana.* Santa Ana, CA: Seven Locks Press, 2000.

Charles Bowden *Down by the River: Drugs, Money, Murder, and Family.* New York: Simon and Schuster, 2002.

Tom Carnwath and Ian Smith *Heroin Century.* New York: Routledge, 2002.

Ted Galen Carpenter *Bad Neighbor Policy: Washington's Futile War on Drugs in Latin America.* New York: Palgrave Macmillan, 2003.

Sean Connolly *Amphetamines (Just the Facts).* Crystal Lake, IL: Heinemann Library, 2000.

Sean Connolly *Marijuana.* Chicago: Heinemann Library, 2002.

Richard Davenport-Hines *The Pursuit of Oblivion: A Global History of Narcotics.* New York: W.W. Norton, 2002.

Douglas J. Davids *Narco-Terrorism: A Unified Strategy to Fight a Growing Terrorist Menace.* Ardsley, NY: Transnational Publishers, 2002.

Robert L. Dupont and Betty Ford *The Selfish Brain: Learning from Addiction.* Washington, DC: Hazelden Information Education, 2000.

Larry K. Gaines and Peter B. Kraska *Drugs, Crime, and Justice.* Prospect Heights, IL: Waveland Press, 2003.

James P. Gray *Why Our Drug Laws Have Failed and What We Can Do About It: A Judicial Indictment on the War on Drugs.* Philadelphia: Temple University Press, 2001.

Mike Gray, ed. *Busted: Stone Cowboys, Narco-Lords and Washington's War on Drugs.* New York: Thunder's Mouth Press/Nation Books, 2002.

Glen Hanson, Peter Venturelli, and Annette E. Fleckenstein, eds. *Drugs and Society.* Boston: Jones and Bartlett, 2001.

Douglas Husak *Legalize This: The Case for Decriminalizing Drugs.* New York: Verson, 2002.

Janet E. Joy, Stanley J. Watson Jr., and John A. Benson Jr., eds. *Marijuana and Medicine: Assessing the Science Base.* Washington, DC: National Academy Press, 1999.

217

Robin Kirk   *More Terrible than Death: Massacres, Drugs, and America's War in Colombia*, New York: PublicAffairs, 2003.

Timothy Lynch, ed.   *After Prohibition: An Adult Approach to Drug Policies in the 21st Century*. Washington, DC: Cato, 2000.

Robert J. MacCoun and Peter Reuter   *Drug War Heresies: Learning from Other Vices, Times, and Places*. New York: Cambridge University Press, 2001.

Alison Mack and Janet Joy   *Marijuana as Medicine?: The Science Beyond the Controversy*. Washington, DC: National Academy Press, 2000.

Charles F. Manski, John V. Pepper, and Carol V. Petrie, eds.   *Informing America's Policy on Illegal Drugs: What We Don't Know Keeps Hurting Us*. Washington, DC: National Academy Press, 2001.

Bill McCollum, ed.   *Medical Marijuana Referenda Movement in America*. Washington, DC: DIANE Publishing, 2001.

Brian Preston   *Pot Planet: Adventures in Global Marijuana Culture*. New York: Grove Atlantic, 2002.

Ed Rosenthal and Steve Kubby   *Why Marijuana Should Be Legal*, New York: Thunder's Mouth Press, 2003.

Dan Shapiro   *Mom's Marijuana*. New York: Vintage Books, 2001.

Lonny Shavelson   *Hooked: Five Addicts Challenge Our Misguided Rehab System*. New York: New Press, 2001.

Jacob Sullum   *Saying Yes: In Defense of Drug Use*. New York: JP Tarcher, 2003.

Samuel Walker   *Sense and Nonsense About Crime and Drugs: A Policy Guide*. Belmont, CA: Wadsworth, 2000.

Brett Alan Weinberg and Bonnie K. Bealer   *The World of Caffeine: The Science and Culture of the World's Most Popular Drug*. New York: Routledge, 2001.

Index

Abrahamson, Daniel, 138
adolescents
  drug use among, 38, 39–40
  troubled, relationship between drugs
    and, 180–81, 191–92
Afghanistan, as source of opium supply,
  79–80
African Americans
  arrests for drug offenses among,
    60–61
  disenfranchisement of, 62
  traffic violations among, 71
alcohol
  deaths from, 147
  use of, by U.S. twelfth-graders, 39
American Civil Liberties Union
  (ACLU), 70
American Medical Association, position
  of, on medical marijuana, 23
American Psychological Association, on
  DARE program, 120, 124
Anderson, Bruce, 166, 172
Anti-Drug Abuse Act (1988), successes
  and failures in goals of, 29–30
Armentano, Paul, 121
arrests, drug
  drug courts have caused increase in,
    136–37
  for possession vs. dealing, 57
  in 2001, 55
Aum Shinrikyo, 86

Ballance, Cindy, 119
Belenko, Steven, 31, 33
Bennett, William J., 43, 46, 183
  on typical drug user, 61
Benson, John A., Jr., 143, 182
Bias, Len, 113
bin Laden, Osama, 77, 80, 94
Bloom, Allan, 189
Boyd, Graham, 138
Brookhiser, Richard, 190
Brothers, Fletcher, 22
Buckley, William F., Jr., 37, 190
Bush, George H.W., 27, 123
Bush, George W., 23, 94, 177
  on racial profiling, 67
Bush administration, on Canada's
  marijuana decriminalization, 11

Calixte, Denese, 114
Campbell, Tom, 37
Canada, decriminalization of marijuana
  in, 10–12
cannabis. *See* marijuana

Cannabis Reform Law (Canada), 11
Castagna, Carlos, 83
Casteel, Steven, 94
Clinton, Bill, 39, 43, 123
Clinton administration, drug
  enforcement budget of, 34
cocaine
  Colombian narco-terrorism and,
    82–83
  crack
    mandatory minimum sentencing
      and, 113
    vs. powder, racial bias in sentencing
      for, 62–63
  decline in use of, 36, 38
  profitability of, 89
  seizures of, 21
Colombia, narco-terrorism in, 80–83,
  91
Comprehensive Drug Abuse Prevention
  and Control Act (1970), 202
*Conant vs. ONDCP, DOJ, DEA, and
  HHS*, 206
Congressional Black Caucus, 64
Constantine, Thomas A., 48
courts. *See* drug courts
crack cocaine. *See* cocaine
crime
  drugs lead to, 153–54
  nonviolent, mandatory minimum
    sentences cause increase in
    imprisonment for, 64
  war on drugs has reduced, 51

Davids, Douglas J., 95
Davidson, Todd, 115
decriminalization
  European model of, 19–20
  vs. legalization of drugs, 148, 183
Drug Abuse Resistance Education
  (DARE), 102
  reduces drug use, 117–20
    con, 121–24
drug courts
  are a solution to drug problem,
    125–33
    con, 134–40
  cost effectiveness of, 128
  expansion of, 133
    argument for, 23–24
  key elements of, 127
  possible perils of, 131–32
  take resources from voluntary
    treatment programs, 138–39
Drug Enforcement Administration

219